A VISION FOR TEACHING

A Vision for Teaching

Education for Spiritual Growth

George Janvier

AFRICA CHRISTIAN TEXTBOOKS

2018

A Vision for Teaching
Education for Spiritual Growth
© 2018 George Janvier

Africa Christian Textbooks (ACTS)

ACTS Bookshop, International HQ, TCNN,
PMB 2020, Bukuru, Plateau State, 930008, Nigeria
GSM: +234 (0) 803-589-5328; E-mail: pa@actsnigeria.org
Website: http://actsnigeria.org

ISBN: 9789789053902 Print
ISBN: 9789789053919 ePub
ISBN: 9789789053926 Mobi

DEDICATION

This book is dedicated to the next generation of teachers who teach on higher levels of learning and spiritual growth. Their impact is great. May they bear fruit unto eternity for the glory of God. Amen!

CONTENTS

ACKNOWLEDGMENTS

The writer is thankful to the Lord for the encouragement he received through the Diploma, Bachelors, Masters, and PhD students at the ECWA Jos Theological Seminary (JETS). You all have been used by the Lord to help form my philosophy of teaching and impacted my spiritual life.

I was influenced, principally, by two teachers when I was a student of education in the USA. Those men were Professor Jim Pluddemann and Professor Ted Ward. I owe a lot to these men.

Thank you Dr. Don Hall and Dr. Paul Todd for your help in editing this book. Paul you do a wonderful job of supporting the book ministry of ACTS.

May the Lord bless you all. Amen.

CHAPTER 1

UNDERSTANDING ADULT EDUCATION

This book is about a vision for quality education. It is also about higher level teaching of young adults and adults in general. Teaching children and youth would require a separate book. This book is about teaching adults. There is a lot of discussion about who is an adult. Some say when people marry they become adults. However, what about people who never marry? Do they remain youths for their whole lives? Some try to put an age criteria on adults. That causes a lot of controversy as different areas have different cultural understandings of who is an adult and at what age they become adults. For the purpose of this book, I want to define an adult as one who is in Bible school, seminary or graduate school. This includes married students and single students as well. People who attend Bible College, seminary, and graduate school are not children; they are adults preparing for a life's work. The focus and vision of this book is to prepare men and women to teach on the Bible College, seminary and graduate level.

Pedagogy and Andragogy

We begin with a comparison of pedagogy and andragogy. Studying pedagogy helps us to clarify andragogy.

Pedagogy

Pedagogy originally meant the teaching of children. However, today it has taken on a wider meaning.

> Pedagogy is the art, science and practice of teaching. It refers to the profession of teaching, especially systemized learning or instruction in principles and methods of teaching.
> —Barbara Wilkerson in Anthony 2001. p.528

Pedagogy is a system of teaching that has been used for hundreds of years and continues to this day. It refers to systems of instruction and is teacher-centred. It can refer to a system of education that moves learning from theory to practice. It is a system that believes knowing comes first and leads to changes in behaviour. Pedagogy is often related to teaching children but it also can be described as a philosophy of teaching where knowledge is foundational to a student's success.

> The goal of education is the advancement of knowledge and the dissemination of truth.
> **—Former President John F. Kennedy**
> **in; https://www.brainyquote.com**

Andragogy

Andragogy refers to the teaching of adults. "Andragogy is the art and science of helping adults learn." (Gregory C. Carlson in: *Anthony 2001. p.46*). The father of modern andragogy was Dr. Malcolm Knowles. Andragogy follows a different approach to education. Some key elements of Dr. Knowles approach to education include;

- Education that is more self-directed
- Education that is based more on student needs

- Education that is life and reality centred
- Internally motivated, that is, student centred

Further study of Knowles can be done through books on adult education and on the Internet.

Adult Education

When we think of teaching adults, we have to think of two different educational contexts; the college and the church. Both contexts have adults in them but the context of school and church are different.

The importance of teaching adults

Who are adults? Adults are leaders in government, business, schools, church and the home. A group of well-trained adults can make or break any organization, church or family.

- A loving husband makes for a peaceful home.
- A mature pastor makes for a growing church.
- An honest politician provides a peaceful environment for all the people.
- A wise teacher provides a good example.

Adults make things happen. Almost all the people in the Bible were adults. Some were good and some were bad but all had an impact on the people around them. Adults are responsible for the well-being of the people they minister to.

> With adulthood comes responsibility.
> —**Mary L. Simonsen in: https:// www.goodreads.com**

Therefore, adults are leaders. Some adults are leaders before they come to school. Some are leaders while they attend college. Most are leaders after they leave college. While at the college, they are preparing for a life of service as government workers, pastors, teachers, business people, husbands and wives. Adult education makes an impact on them all.

Problems of teaching adults

There are a number of problems associated with teaching adults both in the school and in the church. In the college, both younger and older adults may lack self-confidence. They fear failure on exams and papers. Maybe their secondary school experience was not a good experience and they fear the next level. Older adults who return for advanced degrees complain that they have been out of formal studies for a few years and find it hard to get back into the classroom and the assignments mentality.

College adults also face competition with their fellow students. Some students want to be number one in the class and this intimidates and discourages other students. Finances can be a problem for older returning students. They have a family with children in school who need school fees. Adults face relocation to another part of the country if they want to return as full time students. That means they have to leave their homes, area, and often their families. They are apart from their families for long periods of time. Some adults struggle over accommodations in the school environment. They go from a nice home to a noisy crowded dorm room.

> Most of us never stop to consider our blessings; rather, we spend the day only thinking about our problems. Be grateful for the opportunity to have them.
>
> **—(Bernie Siegal in: https:// www.brainyquote.com)**

Church adult problems are different. Attendance is not required at church. People simply show up, sit, listen and go home afterwards. If they miss a week or two, to them, it does not really matter. Lack of motivation may be a problem. Illiteracy can also be a problem for Sunday school adults. What percentage of the Sunday school class is illiterate? Teachers may not be fully qualified to teach but they volunteer when the pastor makes an appeal for teachers. Usually, in Sunday school, there are no materials to study from, no handouts, no quizzes, no homework and no exams.

Case study #12

Some years ago, I knew a Christian attorney who was appointed by the church board to be chairman of the adult education program. He was perfectly willing to oversee the program. He was willing to teach. He was a good teacher. However, he was completely unwilling to take a course. I asked him why. "I learned everything I need to know about the Christian faith when I was a kid in Sunday school," he replied. "Now I'm an adult and the challenge is to live what I already know." To him adult education was remedial, for adults who somehow missed getting a Christian education when they were younger.

This is not an uncommon view. It arises, in part, from the common attitude toward all education in our culture,

that schooling is something you do when you are young. At a certain point, you graduate and you are all done with education. Even worse, the attitude upon graduation may be thank goodness I don't have to do that anymore!
—http://www.christianitytoday.com/biblestudies/articles/
churchhomeleadership/060118.html?start=1.

This case study highlights some of the mentalities that there are concerning adult education in the church.

> Being reminded about the incredible power of God's love, and living as He intended, is the most powerful motivation to change.
> **—Rick Warren in: https://**
> **www.brainyquote.com**

Adult motivation for learning

Teaching adults in the classroom is a rewarding experience for the teacher as well as the students. The students are in school so they can find employment after graduation. The adult student is a hungry learner as success in the classroom often translates into success in the work-ministry world. Adult students are motivated to learn as it impacts them directly as they seek employment and then commence work-ministry.

In the church adults are motivated as well but for different reasons. No one attends Sunday school so they can find employment somewhere. Their motives are different but equally valid as school-adults. Church-adults attend Sunday school, worship services, discipleship opportunities and Bible studies for the following reasons;

• Learn more about God and their faith.

- Learn more about the Bible.
- Learn more about how to be a better husband or wife.
- Be part of the Christian community.

Characteristics of adult learners

Characteristics of adults in schools are different than adults in the church. Some of the characteristics are;

- Motivation. School adults are motivated to learn as it relates to their future employment.
- Energy. School adults have energy for studies. Work, community, or business concerns do not distract them.
- Attention span. School adults have a good attention span and can listen to longer lectures and class discussions.
- Reading. School adults are readers. Sometimes they are readers because they are required to read. In general, however , these adults like to read.
- Research. School adults have to do research. This is for term papers or thesis writing.
- Chapel. School adults like chapel as it is a break from class lectures and is often challenging, encouraging and motivational by means of preaching and praying.

Characteristics of adults in church are different from adults in the college. Some of the characteristics are:

- Attention span. Often church adults have a shorter attention span than college adults do. They are not used to long teaching sessions and are happy with a one hour Sunday school.
- Motivation. Church adults can be less motivated to listen and learn as the Sunday school lesson does not always relate to their lives.

- Energy. Church adults face many pressures out in the world from work, family, relatives, and regulations.
- They enjoy the worship service if it is lively although they rarely take any notes during the sermon.
- They rarely get homework to do and if the Sunday school teacher assigns reading, they often do not do it.
- Experience. Church adults have a lot of experience in living. This includes experience in the family, community, work, and dealing with the government. If called upon to illustrate a teaching point they have a vast amount of stories to share.

> In the Church of Jesus Christ there can and should be no non-theologians.
> **—Karl Barth in: https://www.brainyquote.com**

How to teach college adults

The following are suggestions for helping college adults have a better educational experience.

- Creative lectures: Lectures should be more than reading a paper or watching a video. Be creative in how you approach the traditional lecture.
- Questions and answers: Involve students in active learning through asking questions. From their answers come other questions and experiences. A teacher will not know if the students are understanding the lecture if the teacher never asks them to reflect on the topic.

- Debates: Debates are a good way to create classroom excitement. This gives students, either individually or as a group, opportunities to research their position and clearly explain their position.
- Reflection papers: reflection papers should be short and not contain scholarly quotes. The teacher is asking the students what the topic means to them.
- Student presentations: Student presentations forces a student to think deeper about a topic. To teach means to learn twice.
- Small groups: Small groups gives students a chance for leadership and the opportunity to learn from each other.
- Written assignments: The traditional term paper and exam can be a good learning tool when used effectively. Be sure and give clear instructions as to what you want in terms of content and presentation.
- Short handouts: Students spend a lot of money on school fees and should get something for it. Short handouts reduces the student's need to write down everything the teacher says. It also gives the student a written paper that they can review after class.
- Respect your students: Today's students are tomorrow's leaders, pastors, missionaries, husbands, wives, and administrators. Respect them as students and they will remember you for a long time to come and learn to respect others.
- Encourage students: Encourage students who fall behind or do poorly on exams. Seek to find out and remediate the problem they have.

How to teach church adults

Teaching church adults has some different priorities. For example:

- Encourage reading: People grow intellectually by reading. Reading opens new worlds to people that they cannot get elsewhere. Jesus read the Bible every week in his synagogue. Luke writes,

> *He* (Jesus) *went to Nazareth, where he had been brought up, and on the Sabbath day he went into the synagogue, as was his custom. He stood up to read, and the scroll of the prophet Isaiah was handed to him. Unrolling it, he found the place where it is written . . .*
>
> —Luke 4:16-17

- Give small homework assignments. Church adults are not used to getting homework assignments. Small assignments will encourage them to study and share what they learned.

- Relate the lessons to life. Sunday school lessons should relate to their lives and not be too theoretical or abstract.

- Train for church positions such as elders, Sunday school teachers, disciplers, and positions of service.

- Simple Handouts: Church adults are not used to getting simple handouts. These handouts will help them remember the lesson and do studies on their own at home.

- Have the pastor visit the class now and then. People like it when the pastor visits the class and makes a few comments on the lesson at hand.

- Ask the class members what they would like to study. This gives the members some ownership in what subjects are going to be taught.

> I am also actively involved in my church and its community activities. We have programmes to improve the lives of our congregation and programmes of outreach in the community.
>
> **—Samuel Wilson in: https:// www.brainyquote.com**

In an important summary quote on andragogy, the writer lists his view of the important points of adult education.

Andragogy asserts that adults learn best when:

- They feel the *need* to learn.
- They have some input into what, why, and how they learn.
- The learning's content and processes have a meaningful relationship to the learner's *past experience.*
- Their experience is used as a learning resource.
- What is to be learned relates to the individual's current life situation and tasks.
- They have as much autonomy as possible.
- The learning climate minimizes anxiety and encourages freedom to experiment.
- Their learning styles are taken into account.
- There is a cooperative learning climate.
- We create mechanisms for mutual planning.
- We arrange for a diagnosis of learner needs and interests and enable the formulation of learning objectives based on the diagnosed needs and interests.
- We design sequential activities for achieving the objectives. https://web.njit.edu/~ronkowit/teaching/andragogy.htm

Conclusion

Teaching adults includes two different groups of adults. First is school-adults in Bible College, seminary and graduate schools. The second group is church-adults. Their characteristics are different and their goals for education are different. A good teacher studies his or her audience and makes the lesson fit the group they are teaching.

Adults are a joy to teach and your impact as a teacher can be great as adults either are leaders in the making or are already leaders. Your influence goes far beyond the classroom or Sunday school class and goes out into the society where the real fruit of your labours will bear fruit.

Study Questions

1. List some different characteristics between college-adults and church-adults.
2. Why is it important to teach adults?
3. What are a few differences between pedagogy and andragogy?

CHAPTER 2

A VISION FOR TEACHING

A few years ago, a pastor came to visit me. He had been one of my students in seminary a few years earlier. He said,

> Sir, what you shared about preaching in class that day changed my approach to preaching and my life. I want to thank you for such a great lesson in class that day.

This is what motivates me to be a teacher; changed lives. I have a vision for students and how God can use me to influence men and women who are headed for greater purposes in their Christian life and service for God.

What is a vision for teaching? Why do some teachers seem to communicate better than other teachers? Why is it that when some teachers teach it makes me want to be a teacher? The difference in teachers is that some teachers have a vision for the art and science of teaching. They love the teaching ministry and work at being better teachers. A vision for teaching is a drive or motivation to be the best communicator they can be. A visionary teacher sees what the students can become and not what they are.

This book has two main themes. First is how to be a better more visionary teacher. This could include all levels of teaching but especially on the Bible College, seminary or university levels. The second theme is how to use the teachings of this book to effect spiritual growth. The goal of all our research, writing and teaching is to see men and women learn how to grow spiritually and pass that learning onto their students. The ultimate final goal of our teaching is that our lives will be lived for the glory of God. We educate for glory not for position. We educate beyond the present. We educate for eternity.

> A teacher affects eternity; he or she can never tell where his influence stops.
> **—Proverb in Draper p.602**

The High Calling of a Teacher

The teaching profession is one of the highest callings in life a person can receive. Where would we be without teachers? Who has progressed in life without a teacher or teachers? This section will explore spiritually gifted teachers and people who volunteer themselves to the teaching profession.

Spiritual gifts play a major role in the life of the church, school and individual Christian.

> A spiritual gift is spiritual in character, given by God the Holy Spirit, to others, in the power of God, with an evident manifestation of the Holy Spirit, through the Christian as he or she serves God.
> —Jerry Falwell and Elmer Towns in Stepping out on Faith p.127 in:http://www.sermonillustrations.com/a-z/s/ spiritual_gifts.htm

Two Types of Teachers

There are two types of teachers in the church and Christian colleges today. The first is the Holy Spirit gifted teacher. These teachers see more spiritual fruit and results than other teachers do. The Holy Spirit gifted teacher speaks more to the soul and spirit of the students. Every Christian is specially gifted by the Holy Spirit for specific ministry work. Not all Christians have the spiritual gift of teaching. All Christians have at least one special gift that empowers them for supernatural ministry. The power of a spiritual gift lies with the Holy Spirit and not the individual. The gifted evangelist sees more fruit than the average Christian. The person with the gift of giving is able to give sacrificially with greater joy. The Holy Spirit gifted teacher will see more fruit from his or her teachings. According to Ephesians 4:11 Jesus gives gifts to individuals. The passage says, *"So Christ himself gave the apostles, the prophets, the evangelists, the pastors and teachers."* The gifted teacher comes from God.

Everyone's a Teacher

The second type of teacher is the Hebrews 5:12 teacher where the writer to the Book of Hebrews says, *By this time you ought to be teachers.* This verse represents all Christians who are maturing and need to pass on what they have learned to others. The Great Commission backs this up where it says,

> *Therefore, go and make disciples of all nations, baptizing them in the name of the Father and of the Son and of the Holy Spirit, and teaching them to obey everything I have commanded you. And surely I am with you always, to the very end of the age.*
>
> —Matthew 28:19-20

This command of Jesus is not only for missionaries but also for all Christians. The task here is educational. Jesus said to go into all the world and do two educational tasks. First to make disciples. The second to teach them to obey the commands of Jesus. Making disciples and teaching them is for all Christians, not just the gifted teachers. There is room in the body of Christ for both the spiritually gifted teacher and the volunteer teacher.

Teachers and the Glory of God

Both the gifted teacher and other teachers are to focus on the glory of God. This means to live and act in all ways that honours God and testifies to our trust in him. What does it mean to give God glory? It means to praise, magnify and honour God in worship.

> *All the nations you have made will come and worship before you, O Lord; they will bring glory to your name. For you are great and do marvellous deeds; you alone are God.*

> —Psalm 86:9-10

Second, to glorify God means to speak of him in a truthful way so we can worship him in the beauty of his holiness, truth and love. Third, to glorify God means to honour him with our mouth, mind, and acknowledge his greatness, faithfulness, righteousness and worthiness.

Volunteers and Being Called

Christians are to volunteer for service as teachers (Note the Great Commission's command to make disciples and to teach the things Jesus commanded). Nevertheless, teaching is also a special calling for some teachers.

Case study #1

My own teaching career began as a volunteer. I had never taught much until I was posted to a Bible school and was given several classes to teach. I began my journey as a volunteer and through those courses that I taught, I felt God calling me to teach. I also felt that teaching became my gift as I had a real vision for the classroom and students and saw spiritual fruit from my teaching. Sometimes God's call comes before we take a step of faith and sometimes the call comes after we take a step of faith.

> As a teacher, you become good at maximizing the best in people to bring out their greatest assets.
>
> —http://bigthink.com

The gifts and calling of a teacher are by faith in God and his promises to equip every Christian for service. Some have the special gift of teaching. Romans 12: 6-7 says, *"We have different gifts, according to the grace given to us. If your gift is . . . teaching, then teach."*

Not every Christian is a gifted teacher but all Christians are called to do teaching activities such as making disciples and teaching people to obey the commands of Jesus.

There are many good sayings concerning teachers and teaching. Here are a few;

"As a general rule, teachers teach more by what they are than by what they say." (McKenzie p.501)

"The mediocre teacher tells. The good teacher explains. The superior teacher demonstrates. The great teacher inspires." (McKenzie p.501)

"Good teachers know how to bring out the best in students." (Charles Kuralt in: biblereasons.com)

"The influence of a good teacher can never be erased." (http://biblereasons.com/teachers/)

These sayings all point to the need for high quality teachers who have a vision for the impact they can have on the students they teach. The teacher on the higher level should feel especially fulfilled as he or she is teaching the next generation of leaders, speakers, thinkers and writers. Teachers on the higher level launch men and women into significant ministries both in the church and in a variety of school settings both Christian and secular.

The Bible on Teaching

Scripture is the foundational textbook on what it means to be a teacher. We will look at what the Bible says about teaching and teachers from a variety of Old and New Testament verses.

The Old Testament on Teaching

Old Testament kings, prophets, priests and parents were the teachers in the days of the Old Testament. Schools, or colleges, as we think of them today, were a much later invention. There was one school mentioned in the Old Testament and that was the "School of the Prophets." When you think of the word "school" in the Old Testament context, don't think of things such as school fees, exams, lecturers, and other items associated with schools in the twenty first century. In the school of the prophets, the Holy Spirit was the teacher and the curriculum. The only exams were when the prophecy came true or not. The school of the prophet is mentioned in 1 Samuel 19:18-24 and 2 Kings 2.

> There were at least three schools or communities of these prophets and possibly more, consisting of men who were devoted to God and served Him. They followed the teachings of Samuel, Elijah, and Elisha during the time of the prophets and were known as their "students."
>
> —(https://www.gotquestions.org/school-of-prophets.html)

On a day-to-day basis, most education was done in the home by the parents. Proverbs 22:6 echoes this statement. *Train up a child in the way he should go and when he is old, he will not depart from it.*

Old Testament Verses on Teaching for Today

The Bible is as rich today as it was when the words were originally given. Several teaching verses come to mind from the Old Testament. They are:

> *Let my teaching fall like rain and my words descend like dew, like showers on new grass, like abundant rain on tender plants.*
>
> —Deuteronomy 32:2

Farmers in an agrarian culture are dependent on rains for their crops. Teaching is supposed to be a blessing to the students like rain is to a farmer. Be a "Farmer-teacher" and plant seeds that will bear much fruit.

> *The hearts of the wise make their mouths prudent, and their lips promote instruction. Gracious words are a honeycomb, sweet to the soul and healing to the bones.*
>
> —Proverbs 16:23-24

Teacher's words should be sweet to the students. Harsh judgmental teaching is not tasty and discourages student learning.

Exodus 4:12: *Now go; I will help you speak and will teach you what to say.* Teaching has a supernatural element to it as God empowers the words of the teacher. Teachers need to pray in advance so that God will use them in the classroom.

> *They read from the Book of the Law of God, making it clear and giving the meaning so that the people understood what was being read.*
>
> —Nehemiah 8:8

One of the important goals of a teacher is clear communication. Teachers need to seek to "express" rather than "impress" students. Nehemiah's goal was clear communication of the Bible he was teaching. Sometimes we over teach students. This means we try to do too much teaching and not enough application or interaction.

Sometime less is more. It is better to have students remember a few things than forget many things.

Job 34:4: *Let us discern for ourselves what is right; let us learn together what is good.* Students have the ability to think for themselves. On the higher level of teaching, we need to encourage them to think and apply our teachings to their own lives.

Psalm 32:8: *I will instruct you and teach you in the way you should go; I will counsel you with my loving eye on you.* Teachers do more than pass on information to students. They instruct and counsel students in making life decisions. This is the ministry of the Holy Spirit as well. Jesus said he would send the Holy Spirit to teach us all things and to counsel us as part of his ministry in our lives.

Proverbs 24:32: *I applied my heart to what I observed and learned a lesson from what I saw.* Students on higher levels come with a wide scope of life experiences. The good teacher uses these experiences for the benefit of all the students in the classroom.

New Testament verses on Teaching for Today

There are many verses in the New Testament on being a teacher. A few of them are as follows;

> *When they did not find him (Jesus), they went back to Jerusalem to look for him. After three days, they found him in the temple courts, sitting among the teachers, listening to them and asking them questions.*
>
> —Luke 2:45-46

Jesus, as the student, asked questions of the teachers and leaders of that day. Teachers should not look down or laugh at the questions of students. There is no such thing as a bad question.

Luke 6:40: *The student is not above the teacher, but everyone who is fully trained will be like their teacher.* If students become like you what will they be like? Teachers need to be examples of what they want the students to become.

1 Timothy 4:7: *Have nothing to do with godless myths and old wives' tales; rather, train yourself to be godly.* This verse has two main ideas in it. First, we are to avoid myths, tales, rumours, doubts and philosophies. They waste time and do not contribute much to helping students discover truth. Second, people have the ability to train themselves. Teachers need to teach students how to discover truth for themselves.

> *Do your best to present yourself to God as one approved, a worker who does not need to be ashamed and who correctly handles the word of truth.*
>
> —2 Timothy 2:15

As teachers, we are responsible to do the work of discovering truth before passing on our discoveries to the students. Second, we ultimately work for God not the college or students. Therefore, you need to study and present your information wisely and accurately.

> *In everything set them an example by doing what is good. In your teaching show integrity, seriousness and soundness of speech that cannot be condemned.*
>
> —Titus 2:7

The life of a teacher is a life of example. As the proverb says, "Character comes before the teacher." Our character follows us around whether we like it or not. Every teacher develops a teaching persona and students notice that personal character of the teacher. James 3:2 echoes this theme saying, *Not many of you should become teachers, my brothers, for you know that we who teach will be judged with greater strictness.* This verse should not discourage us from becoming teachers but should challenge us to study, pray, research, read and be well prepared when we enter the classroom.

The Supernatural in Teaching

The supernatural ministry of the Holy Spirit plays a big part in the success of our teaching. For example;

> *But the Advocate, the Holy Spirit, whom the Father will send in my name, will teach you all things and will remind you of everything I have said to you.*
>
> *—John 14:26*

This verse is a key verse in the success of your teaching. The Holy Spirit empowers the teacher in the ministry. Rely on and acknowledge the Holy Spirit in your classroom.

> *This is what we speak, not in words taught us by human wisdom but in words taught by the Spirit, explaining spiritual realities with Spirit-taught words.*
>
> *—1 Corinthians 2:13*

The true teacher of spiritual truth is the Holy Spirit. Teachers use human words but the Spirit uses spiritual language. The Spirit convicts students of truth and is the ultimate teacher of truth.

> *I did not receive it from any man, nor was I taught it; rather I received it by revelation from Jesus Christ.*
>
> *—Galatians 1:12*

There is book learning and there is Jesus learning. Both should take place in the Christian classroom. Jesus learning comes through prayer and a teacher's walk and reliance on Jesus for the true teachings that a teacher needs.

> *Because our gospel came to you not simply with words but also with power, with the Holy Spirit and deep conviction. You know how we lived among you for your sake.*
>
> *—1 Thessalonians 1:5*

Teachers speak many words in every classroom. However, the convicting power of the Holy Spirit is what changes students' lives. Also, note that the apostle Paul lived among his followers. Students need to see how their teachers live.

Curriculum Priorities

Curriculum priorities means the goals we are to strive for as teachers. A saying goes, that if you aim at nothing you will hit it every time. What are we to aim for as teachers? Here are five emphasizes we are to aim for as teachers;

The Glory of God

The glory of God is the great theme of the Bible. Honouring God with our lives and ministries is the great goal of our teaching. The glory of God relates to our work as teachers. John 17:4 says, *I have brought you glory on earth by finishing the work you gave me to do.* Work glorifies God. Teach as unto the Lord so that he gets the praise for our teaching. 1Corinthians 10:31 echoes this these, *So whether you eat or drink or whatever you do, do it all for the glory of God.* Teaching is included in this as well.

Prayer

Prayer was part of the curriculum of Jesus. In Luke 11:1-2 the disciples came to Jesus and said, *Lord, teach us to pray. Jesus responded saying, When you pray say, Father hallowed be your name your kingdom come.* Prayer was a personal and teaching priority of the Jesus curriculum. Make your classroom a house of prayer.

The Great Commission

The Great Commission says in Matthew 28:19-20,

> *Therefore go and make disciples of all nations, baptizing them in the name of the Father, and of the Son and of the Holy Spirit and teaching them to obey everything I have commanded you. And surely I am with you always, to the very end of the age.*

Teachers need to encourage evangelism and discipleship in their classrooms using stories and illustrations of people who go into all the world and making disciples just as Jesus commanded us to do.

The Great Commandment

The Great Commandment is to love God and love people. Matthew 22:37-40 states,

> *Love the Lord your God with all your heart and with all your soul and with all your mind. This is the first and greatest commandment. And the second is like it: Love your neighbour as yourself. All the Law and the Prophets hang on these two commandments.*

Love should permeate our teaching. Students should see and hear from teachers their love for God, others and students. Harsh judgmental teaching does not show love. Learn to demonstrate your love for God and others in the classroom.

The Church

The church is a priority to Jesus. He said in Matthew 16:18:

> *And I tell you that you are Peter and on this rock I will build my church, and the gates of Hades will not overcome it.*

Teachers need to be church-focused people. Make the application of some of your teachings to be church related. Demonstrate that you are a person who loves the church. Students will follow your example and love for the church.

Maturity

Student maturity is another curriculum goal of our teaching. Students should be more mature after our course is finished than when it began. The maturity should be in terms of helping students become more like Jesus Christ. Paul states one of the great curriculum priorities in Colossians 1:28 saying,

> He (Jesus) *is the one we proclaim, admonishing and teaching everyone with all wisdom, so that we may present everyone fully mature in Christ.*

What can you do to point students in a maturing in Christ direction?

Conclusion

We need a greater vision for the impact a teacher can make. Teaching is a high calling from God. Teaching is more than a job. It is more than getting employment. It is influencing a generation of students to become all they can be in Christ. Take your calling seriously and live for the glory of God and the advancement of the students. Be a visionary teacher.

Study Questions

1. What is the difference between teachers who are called and ones who volunteer?
2. Which of the five curriculum priorities listed above is most difficult to do? Explain your answer.
3. What can you do to point students the direction of maturing in Christ?

CHAPTER 3

JESUS THE AMAZING TEACHER

When we think of successful teachers in the Bible, Jesus has to be considered the number one successful teacher. There has never been a more balanced, holistic and spiritually minded teacher than he was. Jesus was a master teacher with a vision for what he wanted to accomplish in the lives of his disciples.

Case study #2

> Socrates taught for 40 years. Plato for 50. Aristotle for 40, and Jesus for only three years. Yet the influence of Christ's three-year ministry infinitely transcends the impact left by the combined 130 years of teaching from these men who were among the greatest philosophers of all antiquity. Every sphere of human greatness has been enriched by this humble Carpenter of Nazareth.
>
> —Tan p.647

We not only consider Jesus to be a successful teacher today but he was considered an <u>amazing</u> teacher in his own lifetime. Here are a few verses that show how people considered his teaching ministry to be amazing;

> *When Jesus ha∂ finishe∂ saying these things; the crow∂s were amaze∂ at his teaching, because he taught as one who ha∂ authority, an∂ not as their teachers of the law.*
>
> *—Matthew 7:28-29*

Mark 1:27, *The people were all so amaze∂ that they aske∂ each other, "What is this? A new teaching an∂ with authority!"*

> *When the Sabbath came, he began to teach in the synagogue, an∂ many who hear∂ him were amaze∂. "Where ∂i∂ this man get these things?" they aske∂. "What's this wis∂om that has been given him?"*
>
> *—Mark 6:2*

Mark 10:24, *The ∂isciples were amaze∂ at his wor∂s.*

> *The chief priests an∂ the teachers of the law hear∂ this an∂ began looking for a way to kill him, for they feare∂ him, because the whole crow∂ was amaze∂ at his teaching.*
>
> *—Mark 11:18*

Luke 4:22, *All spoke well of him an∂ were amaze∂ at the gracious wor∂s that came from his lips. "Isn't this Joseph's son?" they aske∂?"*

John 7:15, *The Jews there were amaze∂ an∂ aske∂, "How ∂i∂ this man get such learning without having been taught?"*

The people all agreed that he was an amazing teacher. Jesus was recognized as a visionary teacher.

Jesus' vision

What was Jesus' vision as a teacher? He had a vision for what the disciples could become. He set a high example of what a teacher could be. He wanted to train twelve godly men to take the gospel worldwide.

They were to be grounded in Scripture, practical in application, humble and loving in their approach to reaching the world.

> *Jesus went through all the towns and villages, teaching in their synagogues, proclaiming the good news of the kingdom and healing every disease and sickness.*
>
> —Matthew 9:35

Jesus lived and taught the message he wanted the disciples to proclaim.

What Made Jesus an Amazing Teacher?

Although Jesus did pastoral type of work, he was not called a pastor. He did mission work but was not called a missionary. The essential ministry of Jesus was teaching and he was thus called a Rabbi, which means teacher. What was it that made Jesus such an amazing teacher? Let us look at the key passage for this answer. Matthew 7:28-29 says,

> *When Jesus had finished saying these things, the crowds were amazed at his teaching, because he taught as one who had authority, and not as their teachers of the law.*

The context

The context of these two verses is found in the Sermon on the Mount. Matthew 5:1-2 tells us,

> *Now when Jesus saw the crowds, he went up on a mountainside and sat down. His disciples came to him and he began to teach them.*

These verses took place early in the ministry of Jesus. In order to understand Jesus the amazing teacher we need to look at what led up to the Sermon on the Mount. What was Jesus' ministry up to Matthew 5:1? What was he doing?

The ministry record is short. The record is about John the Baptist, the temptation, choosing the disciples, brief ministry in the north of

Israel and then the Sermon on the mouth. For our purposes, the record begins in Matthew 4:12-25.

Jesus' three-fold ministry was teaching, proclaiming and healing. The results were that large crowds followed him.

Before Jesus got to the Sermon on the Mount he established himself with the people as teacher, proclaimer and healer who was concerned with the needs of the people. He was not seen as a rebel and he taught in conventional religious establishments such as the synagogues of the day. He was regarded as a popular speaker who was concerned with the people's spiritual and physical condition. He proclaimed the gospel of the Kingdom not his own kingdom.

Before Jesus said one word of the Sermon on the Mount, he had a popular reputation. People were following him wherever he went. His life and ministry backed up his teachings.

> Jesus had things to say about how we should behave that captivated his listeners and have continued to captivate succeeding generations.
>
> **—Muggeridge in Draper p.352**

Now we come to the Sermon itself. What is the essence of the Sermon on the Mount?

> The Sermon on the Mount is the sermon that Jesus gave in Matthew chapters 5-7. The Sermon on the Mount is the most famous sermon Jesus ever gave, perhaps the most famous sermon ever given by anyone.
>
> The Sermon on the Mount covers several different topics. If we were to try to summarize the Sermon on the Mount in a single sentence, it would be something like this: How to live a life that is dedicated to and pleasing to God, free

from hypocrisy, full of love and grace, full of wisdom and discernment.

—https://www.gotquestions.org/sermon-on-the-mount.html

In Matthew 7:28-29 we learn some things about the context of these two verses. For example, we learn one positive and one negative aspect of the context.

1. Positively Jesus taught as One having authority.
2. Negatively Jesus did not teach like their teachers of the law. (The Scribes).

Teaching with Authority

What does it mean that Jesus taught with authority? What is authority? "Authority" is the power or right to give orders, make decisions and enforce obedience. Other words, which can mean authority, are power, command, control, rule and sovereignty.

Jesus got his authority from God the Father. The Bible says, *Then Jesus came to them and said, "All authority in heaven and on earth has been given to me"* (Matthew 28:18). This verse clearly shows that the authority that Jesus had, came from the Father to the Son. Jesus had the authority to forgive sins (Mark 2:10), to drive out demons (Mark 3:15), to be overcome impure spirits (Mark 6:7), and the authority to give eternal life (John 17:2). He had authority because it was given to him by God, and that fact that he was the Son of God. Jude 1:25 states, *To the only God our Saviour be glory, majesty, power and authority, through Jesus Christ our Lord, before all ages, now and forevermore! Amen.*

Dr. Joe Kapolyo, from Zambia, said,

> His (Jesus) words were not based on reinterpretation of ancient texts, but was the personal authority of an originator. The

crowds, who formed the background to the ministry of Jesus, recognized this.

—African Bible Commentary p.1125

The people were amazed that Jesus spoke with such authority. They had not heard someone teach like this before.

Not as the Scribes

Second, Jesus did not teach as the Scribes. The Scribes were the keepers of the Law in ancient Israel. Their job was to study and copy the manuscripts, which is how the Bible was recorded in those days. They took their job very seriously and realized they were working with the word of God. They were the lawyers of the day often called on to interpret the Law.

The Scribes, though, went beyond their responsibilities as recorders of the Scriptures. They began to add to the Scriptures their own interpretations which slowly became more important that the word of God itself. A large portion of Jesus' sermon then dealt with what the people had been taught by the scribes and what God actually wanted from his people. It came down to a choice between the word of God or the traditions of men. This was revolutionary and shocking to the common people as all their lives they had listened to the Scribes teach on the importance of their traditions.

> Tradition is a guide and not a jailer.
> **—W. Somerset Maugham. http:// www.goodreads.com**

Second, the Scribes were concerned more with the outer man rather than the inner man and his heart. This was teaching on a higher level than what the people were used to. The people were used to the teachings of the Scribes and their emphasis on the external keeping of the Law rather than the inner spiritual life of the heart.

The style of teaching of the Scribes was lecture style. They quoted the experts by saying, "Rabbi so-and-so says this." Their teaching was dull, lifeless, academic, abstract and theoretical with parallels to some religious traditions today. They taught about the Bible but not the Bible itself. The Scribes put all their weight on the Law and its interpreters. It was built on the traditions and interpretations of men.

The Jesus method of teaching was different from that of the Scribes, hence the people were amazed at his teaching. Jesus did not exactly lecture which comes from the word "Legere" which means to read. Why was it not a lecture? The Jesus method was not a lecture for a few reasons. First, he sat with his students. He spoke of practical and philosophical-theological concerns of the disciples. He gave no quiz or notes and he did not read a paper. The Jesus method was a stimulating presentation from the heart not the head. It was not just information and a quiz, it was life giving.

Some teachers today claim that the Sermon on the Mount was a lecture. While it does have a few characteristics of a lecture, it was not an academic presentation like the Scribes would give or that we sometimes see today. It appears that Jesus did all the talking. This was because the disciples were beginners and if they had information, it may have been false information based on the traditions of men and not Scripture. Jesus also conveyed a large body of teaching in a short space of time. The Sermon may be a summary of a larger body of teachings that he may have given. Terry Powell in the *Baker Evangelical Dictionary of Christian Education* states,

> Students' attention increases when lecturers appeal to two
> or more senses, when key concepts are visualized. Their

perception of the contents relevance to their lives is also a crucial motivational variable.

—p. 423

Jesus appealed to more than one of the disciples' senses.

Some Examples of Jesus' Teachings

Teaching consists of "content" and "presentation." Content is the actual information that a teacher is passing on to the students. The presentation is how the material is conveyed from the teacher to the student. The following is some of the content of Jesus' teachings.

Easy to understand

Some of Jesus' teaching was easy for the disciples to understand. Similarly, some of our teaching needs to be introductory and foundational for all to understand. Simpler teaching encourages the students. For example, Jesus said;

- *But when you pray, go into your room, close the door and pray to your Father who is unseen.* (Matthew 6:6).
- *If you forgive men when they sin against you, your heavenly Father will also forgive you.* (Matthew 6:14).
- *But when you fast, put oil on your head and wash your face, so that it will not be obvious to men you are fasting.* (Matthew 6:17).

Hard to understand

Other teaching by Jesus was hard for the disciples to understand. Likewise, not all of our teaching should be spoon-feeding. Tough questions are a part of challenging students to think and wrestle with difficult topics. For example, Jesus taught;

- *If your right eye causes you to sin gouge it out.* (5:29).
- *And lead us not into temptation.* (6:13).

- *An⸗ not everyone who says to me Lor⸗, Lor⸗ will enter the king⸗om of heaven. Many will say to me on that ⸗ay Lor⸗, Lor⸗ ⸗i⸗ we not prophesy in your name. Then I will tell them I never knew you.* (7:21-23).
- *Love your enemies an⸗ pray for those who persecute you.* (5:44)

Holding to a high standard

Jesus dealt with the heart and held people to a high standard of morality. All Christian teaching needs to be held to a high standard of spirituality. For example;

- *Anyone who is angry with his brother is subject to ju⸗gment.* (5:21).
- *Anyone who looks at a woman lustfully has committe⸗ a⸗ultery.* (5:27).
- *Do not store up treasurers on earth.* (6:19).

Jesus encouraged the listeners

Jesus preached a positive message to encourage his listeners. No teacher had probably told them these things before. For example, Jesus taught;

- *Blesse⸗ are the poor in spirit, for theirs is the king⸗om of heaven.* (5:3).
- *You are the salt of the earth, you are the light of the worl⸗.* (5:13-14).
- *Are you not more valuable that the bir⸗s?* (6:26).
- *Go⸗ clothes the grass with he not much more cloth you?* (6:30).
- *Ask an⸗ it shall be given unto you.* (7:7).

Jesus spoke with authority

As we have said before, Jesus spoke with authority and he challenged oral traditions. Oral traditions can be good but when they take over the authority of Scripture a teacher will get into trouble. For example he said,

- *Do not think that I have come to abolish the Law or the Prophets; I have not come to abolish them but to fulfill them.* (5:17).

- *You have heard that it was said to the people long ago, "You shall not murder" . . . but I tell you . . . (5:21-22).*
- *You have heard that it was said, "You shall not commit adultery." But I tell you . . . (5:27-28).*

Jesus spoke about the heart

The Scribes were more concerned about the external keeping of the Law and traditions. Jesus was more concerned about issues of the inner man. For example;

- *For where your treasure is, there your heart will be also. (6:21).*
- *Blessed are the pure in heart, for they will see God. (5:8).*
- *But I tell you that anyone who looks at a woman lustfully has already committed adultery with her in his heart. (5:28).*

> Jesus leaps in a unique way across the changing centuries because he spoke to the unchanging needs of the heart of man.
> **—C.T. Craig in Draper p.352**

Teachers today need to teach more than to the head, they need to teach to the heart.

Things Jesus did not do

Jesus as a teacher did not do a number of things. He did not shout as we do today. He did not read a set of lecture notes or read from a book. He did not quote from many scholars. He did not try to raise money. He did not offer a certificate or degree.

Things Jesus did do

Jesus spoke in a language and style that captured people's attention. He used the Bible as his content. He illustrated his teaching and drew examples from daily life. He spoke about issues that people were interested in. He clarified wrong teaching. People recognized Jesus as a teacher of truth. In Luke 20:21 the people said,

> *Teacher, we know that you speak and teach what is right, and that you do not show partiality but teach the way of God in accordance with the truth.*

All people realized that Jesus was a teacher of truth.

> The essential teachings of Jesus were literally revolutionary and will always remain so if they are taken seriously.
> **—Hebert J. Muller in Draper p.354**

Although in some ways, Jesus appeared like a Jewish rabbi or Greek philosopher instructing his pupils. But Jesus did not come to hand down accepted precepts, whether legal or philosophical. Jesus came with the authority of the reign of God . . . Jesus brought life, not abstract theories. Jesus touched people in their deepest hearts and souls.

—Vernon Blackwood p.686 in the *Evangelical Dictionary of Christian Education* by M. Anthony, 2001

The Authority of the Believer

Where does the authority of the believer come from today? The Christian teacher cannot claim Divine inspiration like Jesus did. The Christian teacher gets his or her authority from one of two places. They get it from relying on the Word of God and the Holy Spirit. "Thus says the Lord" is our authority. Quoting scholars is good but quoting the Scriptures is better.

The authority of the believer comes from God and from his word. As ambassadors of the Lord, we can speak with his authority. Paul wrote, *For you know what instructions we gave you by the authority of the Lord Jesus* (1 Thessalonians 4:2). Our authority comes from the Lord and his word.

How to be an amazing teacher

We need to follow the Jesus model of teaching and not the Scribes. In the negative, they were dry and dull in their classroom approach. They quoted scholars but lacked the Scriptural references to back up their teachings. First, be careful not to read a set of notes. Speak from notes but do not rely completely on them.

Second, challenge conventional thinking. Sometimes ideas become accepted as truth but have no root in the truth. For example, prosperity gospel has some good ideas but is not grounded in holistic truth of the Scriptures.

Third, teach to the inner man, the heart, morals and motives and not just the head.

The Scribes teachings did not really connect with the issues of the day. Let us not teach like the world teaches but be concerned about the inner man (the heart) as well as the mind. Jesus was scholarly but he also told people how to live a godly life pleasing to God. Jesus taught on; how to be blessed, the Kingdom, prayer, giving, marriage and divorce, lawsuits, fasting, heaven and more. He did a lot of application in his teaching. This is not devotional teaching. He corrected wrong thinking. This will help students sharpen their thinking and reasoning. Jesus often said, "You have heard it said, but I say."

Fourth, we need to connect with students through application to the issues they will face in ministry. If you were to enter a classroom today and say, "Today we will teach on how to be blessed, prayer, giving, marriage and divorce, lawsuits, fasting and heaven" you would probably wake up many students. To be an amazing teacher you need to be biblical, be scholarly and connect our teaching with the issues of the day.

Conclusion

In looking at the teaching ministry of Jesus as a whole, what do we see? In summary;

- The teachings of Jesus were revolutionary.
- His teachings were founded on love.
- His teachings go as deep as you allow them to go.
- He taught on the inner soul of people.
- He spoke of the greatness of God.
- He spoke of justice.
- He taught the lowly of society.
- He spoke of the unchanging needs of the human heart.
- He taught on the past, the present and the future.
- He role modelled what he taught.

Follow these principles of Jesus' teaching and people will say you are an amazing teacher.

Study Questions

1. How, as teachers, can we be more like Jesus in our teaching?
2. What aspects of Jesus' life can we not be like?
3. How was Jesus different than the Scribes as a teacher?

CHAPTER 4

TYPES OF TEACHERS

The world is composed of a variety of teachers, some good some not so good, some that lecture and some that teach interactively, some who encourage students to rise higher and some who do not.

Case study #3

A professor of educational philosophy in the USA changed the way I teach. Before that class, I had not truly been challenged about what I actually thought. Much of my education was repeating what the teacher said. This teacher was the first teacher who asked me questions that we did not know the answers to. Realizing that I actually had to provide the answers from within myself, and not look to an outside source was very difficult at first. It was a muscle I had to build. I owe a lot of who I am today to the critical thinking I learned from that teacher.

—Susan Zimmerman in http://blog.ted.com/the-teachers-who-inspired-us-and-even-changed-the-trajectories-of-our-lives/

In order to be a visionary teacher, a teacher needs to both understand the bigger picture of the art and science of teaching, and know where he or she fits into that larger picture. In the classroom, we have various teacher styles and learning styles. For this chapter we will look at teacher styles.

No two teachers teach the exact same way. As teachers, we may "borrow" someone else's style but then we make it our own style of communicating. We need to look at teaching styles and try to determine what teaching style you are.

The first two styles of teaching, under discussion here, are broad in scope as we compare the styles of African and Western teachers. In attempting to compare the styles of African and Western teachers, some generalizations have to be made. Not all African teachers teach the same way. They vary from one area to the next. One person might say, "That is exactly how it is done in my area." Whereas someone from another area, in reading the exact same characteristics of a teacher might say, "That is not how it is done in my area." Therefore, some liberty has to be given in accepting the following as characteristics of the African teacher. (I am attempting to draw from African writers over the Internet and my own experience interacting with seminary students for 25 years in Nigeria).

The traditional African teacher

The traditional African teacher is based in the village of his tribal group. He is an older man who is well respected by the majority of the people in the village. His responsibilities are to pass on the traditions of the tribe including language, customs, marriage and religion. He gathers younger boys around him for informal teaching and rituals of the tribe. Often the ceremonies end with certain rituals that cause the boys to pass from boyhood to manhood.

Several underlying themes guide the teacher in his teaching of the students. They are;

• God is in control

- You cannot change or know the future
- Leave things as they are
- Traditions are important
- Oriented to the past

The traditional teacher has all authority and has power over the students' well-being. Rarely does the teacher abuse the students but discipline is used when necessary.

The teaching methods are traditional, informal, and oral using time tested methods. These methods include such things as music, dance, stories, histories and proverbs.

> There are storytelling traditions that come from Africa that are unique from anywhere else.
>
> **—Elvis Mitchell in: https:// www.brainyquote.com**

Proverbs are short teaching tools that bring a pointed message once the proverb is explained. Here are a few traditional proverbs;

- "The tallest trees take the most wind."
- "They only throw stones at trees that bear fruit."
- "He who stands in the sun will begin to sweat."
- "A knife does not sharpen itself."
- "All fingers are not equal."

The traditional teacher is action oriented as well as information oriented. The information relates to traditions of the tribe but the actions relates to skills that need to be developed. Students told me that it is like an apprenticeship programme, which traditional teachers use to teach a variety of skills that help the students find work and to fit into the tribe. Their presentation is more dramatic and emotional rather than a cold lecture. The historical perspective is more oriented to the past; that is, to tribal history and customs. The traditional teacher has responsibilities to do more than pass on facts. He is responsible to pass on life principles and life traditions. The teacher does not need a building, or a Principal, a library, classrooms, written diplomas, a faculty, time clock or school fees. All youths were able to attend the traditional school.

The Western teacher

It is not the purpose of this book to examine all the possible teaching environments where a western teacher is teaching. Instead the role of a more formal teacher will be examined here. Broad generalizations will be made about the western teacher and there are exceptions to most of the statements given below.

The western teacher is engaged in formal education in a school setting. He or she can be of any age and has to earn his or her respect based on degrees and performance in the classroom. The western teacher is oriented to ideas and passes on information, facts and content that students must learn.

On higher levels, the teacher is more of a facilitator of learning though discussion of ideas in the classroom. The teacher does not have to integrate his or her teaching with other disciplines and tends to be a specialist in one particular area of studies. His or her responsibilities are to convey clearly the ideas and information that the student will be tested on. Due to large classes, the western teacher is often isolated from personal relationships with students. Not all students are capable of attending a particular college, but only those that pass qualifying exams or criteria.

Several themes guide the western teacher. They are:

- Information (knowledge) is important.
- Formal testing is used to determine student learning.
- Formal, informal, and non-formal methods are to be used.
- Students are to be respected.
- Knowing leads to doing.
- Oriented to the future.
- Change is good.

The teaching methods used by western teachers are formal, lecture style, reliant on literature and the use of technology. Stories, proverbs and music are rarely used. Although the western teacher does not teach using proverbs, several proverbs capture the idea of western education. They are:

- "Knowledge is power."
- "Learning is better than house and land."
- "Never stop learning."
- "People learn on their own rather than being force fed."

(http://www.wiseoldsayings.com/knowledge-quotes/)

> The purpose of learning is growth, and our minds, unlike our bodies, can continue growing as we continue to live.
> **—Mortimer Adler in: http:// www.wiseoldsayings.com**

Similarities between the African and Western teacher

There are many similarities between the African traditional teacher and the western teacher.

Case study #4

In class, I like to ask education students, which is more important for the African context, the traditional African teacher or the western teacher. A lively discussion followed this question as students discuss (argue) their idea on this issue. Some students say that because they are Africans they need to follow the A.T.E. (African traditional education) pattern. Other students say that they are in the 21st century and are part of a greater world now and not just their village. I usually conclude this discussion by saying we can learn from both types of teachers and incorporate their styles of teaching in our modern classrooms.

Both the traditional teacher and the western teacher desire that their students learn, grow and help them fit into the community. The training includes both intellectual data and skills training and is designed to help students fit into the greater society. Both types of education have a moral component that teaches right from wrong. Both have certain criteria to show that the students have mastered the necessary material.

Suggestions for combining the two methods

The teacher in the twenty first century needs to combine the two styles of teaching and learning. The African traditional teacher captures the rich heritage of the people as well as taps into the natural style of learning with which students come to college with. The western teacher helps students move into the twenty first century and to interact with education worldwide. The following are suggestions to make teaching more effective for both the traditional education skills and the western skills in teaching:

- Orient to the past as much as the future. God told the Jews over 200 times to "remember" the events of the past and the God who brought them through troubling times. Can it be any different for us? Yet we also face the future every day when we enter a school setting.
- Orient our teaching to the community as much as to the individual. In a classroom setting, I like to ask students, which is more important, the individual or the community. An intense argument ensues with students lining up on both sides of the discussion. Like African culture, Christianity is community based. In Africa, it is the village or the tribe that is important. In Christianity, the church is the important community. The community is important, but on the other hand, each person will have to give account of his or her life to God one day. Reinforcing the community and the individual is important for the modern era teacher.
- Orient to both power encounter and the scientific method. Power encounter refers to the spirit world in which people in Africa grow up. The scientific method refers to the world in which people in the west grow up. Both are important for the modern classroom. The spirit world is close to peoples' experience. The scientific world is the world of the 21st century. Teachers need to help students respect both of these worlds.
- Orient to poverty and wealth. Our context has a lot of both poverty and wealth. From the village setting to the urban setting poverty and wealth are in the front of people's minds. 1 Samuel 2:7 says, *The Lord sends poverty and wealth; he humbles and he exalts.* Teachers need to correct wrong ideas about poverty and wealth among Christians

and give a clearer understanding of what the Bible really says about poverty and wealth.

- Orient to the New Testament as well at the Old Testament. The Old Testament is very popular among people in Africa. Westerners lean in a New Testament direction. Both are necessary for a complete picture of the Christian life.

Case study #5

> When our seminary offered a PhD in biblical studies, we had five applicants. Four of them wanted to do a PhD in the Old Testament and only one wanted to study for a PhD in the New Testament. The OT connects with people in Africa.

The Old Testament contains stories of village living, wars, gods and idols, power encounters, tribalism, priests and kings and many other examples for Christian teachers to draw from. The New Testament has many principles and teachings for how to live the Christian life and how to function in the church.

- Orient to doing as much as knowing. Proper curriculum has both "doing" and "knowing" as part of the programme. In the Christian life knowing and doing work together. The traditional teacher is strong in doing and the western teacher is strong in knowing. James says in 1:22 *But be doers of the word, and not hearers only, deceiving your own selves* (KJV). Jesus and Paul were both brilliant in the Scriptures but were also models of being doers of the word. We need to follow their example.
- Orient to people as much as ideas. Some students are people-oriented in that they live to talk and be with people. Others are quiet and happy to be alone at home studying and wrestling with ideas. Both are needed in the church. Jesus came for people and Paul taught ideas. Let us follow their examples.

Possible Teaching Styles

What are some possible styles of classroom teaching? The following list some of the more common teaching styles that teachers use.

The scholar-teacher

The scholar-teacher is an expert in his or her field. They are renowned for their understanding of their discipline and have specialized in their discipline for many years. Scholars have a vision for their field of studies. One example of a committed scholar;

Case study #6

> My claim is simply that the literary approach is the one necessary way to read and interpret the Bible, an approach that has been unjustifiably neglected. Despite that neglect, the literary approach builds at every turn on what biblical scholars have done to recover the original, intended meaning of the biblical text.
>
> —Leland Ryken https://www.brainyquote.com

The scholar has done advanced studies in his or her field of studies. The scholar tends to do most of the talking in class as they are the experts in their fields. The students hold their knowledge and experience in high regard. They have gone deep into their discipline and have wrestled with problems in that discipline.

Some of the potential problems with a scholar is that they have so much information in their heads that they have a hard time communicating that knowledge. They also have gone very deep into their discipline and may find it unfulfilling to teach on a simpler level. Scholars make friends with books more than with people. They also see life from their perspective. If they are interested in history, they think everyone should be interested in history. They would look at life through their historical studies, as they have tasted the benefits of history. Because students lack foundational work in certain areas of study, the scholar-teacher usually works well in areas of complex theology, Greek, Hebrew and research methods.

The facilitator-teacher

What is a facilitator-teacher? The facilitator-teacher leads the class in an interactive style designed to accomplish specific goals of the course being taught. The facilitator-teacher has goals but is flexible in how to reach those goals. This means the facilitator asks questions and guides the discussion without pushing the conversation too hard in one direction.

Case study #7

> In a class on pastoral leadership, the teacher wanted to discuss solutions to common problems pastors face in the church, such as problems with the youth, divorce, job loss and much more. Rather than lecture giving students easy answers to hard questions the teacher asked students to identify problems pastors face. After discussing the problems pastors face the teacher led in a discussion on solutions to the problems. The students were struggling with answers but collectively they struggled and came up with some solutions. This had more impact on the students than the lecture method where answers were given to the problems pastors face.

The facilitator-teacher has to do research to be prepared for possible discussion questions and points raised by the students. The facilitator usually begins class with a time of introducing the topic and giving some background to the problem to be discussed. He or she uses questions to guide the discussion. A word of caution; using questions in the African context may require some time for the students to adjust into the idea of the teacher asking students questions which lead to discussions.

Case study #8

At the end of the course I was teaching, the students were given evaluation papers to evaluate the teacher and the course. Because I use questions extensively in my classes, one student thought I was not a good teacher. He wrote on his evaluation of me, "The teacher doesn't know anything, all he does is ask us questions."

You need to explain what facilitation is to the students and why you use questions to teach.

Case study #9

When I first started to study education and teaching, I assumed that the lecture method, given by a scholar, was how people were to learn. Then in graduate school, I sat under my first facilitator-teacher. My vision for teaching was transformed from the teacher as scholar to the teacher as a facilitator of self-discovery. Although there is a place for lecturing, a facilitator produces different results.

> Your key responsibility as a facilitator is to create this group process and an environment in which it can flourish, and so help the group reach a successful decision, solution or conclusion.
> —https://www.mindtools.com/pages/article/RoleofAFacilitator.htm

Discussion and asking questions are key components of being a facilitator-teacher. Being a facilitator-teacher works well on many courses especially in courses that are more practical in nature such as education, youth ministry, and missions courses.

The action oriented teacher

The action-oriented teacher is concerned about skills to be developed by the students. The action oriented teacher works well for courses such as practicum based courses like as being attached to a church if you are a pastoral student or youth ministries student. If you are an education student, you are attached to a school. If you are a missions student you are attached to a church planting missionary for a period of time.

If you are teaching a regular semester based course, the action oriented teaching style works well. For example, practical courses such as homiletics, teaching methods, evangelism, and discipleship are all good for the action-oriented teacher. These courses should not be taught only through the lecture method but through skills development in the classroom. These courses are similar to an extended period practicum based course but shorter in duration.

The action-oriented teacher can also be called a "competency based teacher." Competencies are skills that a student develops during his or her course work. Two important quotes follow;

> Action-oriented learning and teaching is the basic requirement to ensure that the learner acquires professional competence as well as key qualifications such as the ability to solve problems. Action-oriented learning and teaching has proved to be a form of education that allows the learner to learn more than only technical knowledge and skills. A requirement for success is

to structure the training and teaching contents in the form of questions and problems.

—Werner Heitmann; http://www.voced.edu.au/

The most important characteristic of competency-based education is that it measures learning. Students progress by demonstrating their competence, which means they prove that they have mastered the knowledge and skills that are called competencies) required for a particular course.

—https://www.huffingtonpost.com

All classes should have a competency-based (action-oriented) component to it. For some classes that may mean a term paper or final exam. For most classes it means some sort of practical skills development.

The technological teacher

The technological teacher is the teacher of the 21st century. He or she uses technology in the classroom. This could include a computer, video projector, the Internet or any other technical gadgets that help to facilitate learning.

The technological teacher is the teacher of the future in the world of education. In our African context, we need to start slowly as we build up the technical knowhow among the teachers that are currently teaching. The budget for equipment may not be there and the electricity to run the equipment may not be stable but we need to make the attempt to convert our classrooms into places of technology. A final thought on being a technology teacher:

As a technology teacher, you give each generation of students the edge they need to compete in an increasingly technological world. Through your passion and interest in this field, you will create a lasting interest among your students, who will soon be developing the future technology for the next generation of students.

—https://www.alleducationschools.com/secondary-education/technology-teacher/

> It is not so much what is poured into the student, but what is planted, that really counts.
>
> **—McKenzie p.301**

Conclusion

Every teacher has a style of classroom teaching. No single style is right for every teacher, class, or context. Teachers should experiment with the various teaching styles to see what the best style for them to use is. The best teachers work on having a variety of styles to be used for different courses they are called upon to teach.

Study Questions

1. Of the four types of teachers described in this chapter, which one do you see yourself most like?
2. Is the technological teacher realistic for the African context? Explain your answer.
3. What is competency-based education?

CHAPTER 5

THE COGNITIVE

The cognitive refers to the intellect, the brain, knowledge, mental skills, the mind or the intellect. The cognitive forms the foundation for two other disciplines, those of the "affect" and the "psycho-motor" which will be discussed in later chapters of this book.

> The cognitive domain involves knowledge and the development of intellectual skills. This includes the recall or recognition of specific facts, procedural patterns, and concepts that serve in the development of intellectual abilities and skills.
>
> —http://www.nwlink.com

One of the foundational tasks of a teacher is to develop the student's ability to think. The brain uses information, along with other educational activities to shape our thinking.

> Cognitive skills are the core skills your brain uses to think, read, learn, remember, reason, and pay attention. Working together, they take incoming information and move it into the bank of knowledge you use every day at school, at work, and in life.
>
> —https://www.learningrx.com/

A seminary student realized the importance and role that books played in his education and intellectual development. One day after class, he said to me, "If you can get me some of the books you recommended I would sell my clothes to buy them." He got the books. Books help train the mind and the mind plays an important part is training Christians for ministry.

The Apostle Paul told the Colossian Christians that, *He (Jesus) is the one we proclaim, admonishing and teaching everyone with all wisdom, so that we may present everyone fully mature in Christ* (Colossians 1:28). With presenting everyone fully mature in Christ as our goal, the question becomes how do we do that? What elements of visionary teaching leads us to present people fully mature in Christ? Maturity needs to be holistic focusing on various aspects of the Christian life. The educational process plays an important role in developing this maturity.

> One of the marks of spiritual maturity is the quiet confidence that God is in control . . . without the need to understand why he does what he does.
>
> **—Swindoll in Draper p.420**

Along with other aspects of human psychology, the mind plays a key role in the development of Christian maturity. Christian author and teacher Dr. Perry Downs says,

> The final purpose of the educational process of the ministry of the church is to change lives. But the mind is not uninvolved with this process. Scripture asserts that part of the transformation is to be in our thinking. If Christian education is to be effective, it must recapture a proper understanding of the role of the mind in spiritual growth.
>
> —Downs 1994. p.60

Developing the mind is only one part of Christian maturity but it does play a foundational role in developing people's thinking about Scripture and God. Scripture has much to say about the mind, thinking and knowledge. Key verses in human development of the mind will be explored in this chapter.

The renowned American educator, Dr. Benjamin Bloom, shows us how we can build upon a knowledge base in ways that will help us lead others to maturity in Christ. But more about Dr. Bloom later. Because the Word of God is all-important, we will first look at what the Scriptures tell us about the Cognitive, about knowledge.

The Bible on the Development of the Mind

The Apostle Paul gives us a key verse to explore about the Christian mind in Romans 12:2,

> *Do not conform to the pattern of this world, but be transformed by the renewing of your mind. Then you will be able to test and approve what God's will is, his good, pleasing and perfect will.*

> The difference between worldliness and godliness is a renewed mind.
> **—Lutzer in Draper p.424**

Paul says that the renewing of the mind is the foundation of success in overcoming the patterns of this worldly system.

> Our thinking must be changed (transformed) from old, ungodly ways of thinking into new, godly ways of thinking. What we know in our minds to be true forms a conviction

in our hearts of that truth, and that conviction in our hearts translates into action. Therefore, we must first renew our minds. The only way to replace the error of the world's way of thinking is to replace it with God's truth. As Jesus prayed to the Father,

Sanctify them in the truth: your word is truth
(John 17:17).

—https://www.gotquestions.org

Paul tells the Ephesian Christians, *to be renewed in the attitude of your minds* (Ephesians 4:23). The mind needs to be renewed. We were born as sinners and learned sinful ways from our youth onwards. When we were born-again, we had to learn a completely new way of living. Our priorities change in many ways. The food for the change is using God's word to renew our minds. To Paul, the mind played an important way of renewing us to what God wants us to be.

To the Colossian Christians, Paul gave a way of renewing their minds by focusing on God's priorities. He said, *Set your minds on things above, not on earthly things* (Colossians 3:2). So what are the things above? They are God and his glory, the Kingdom of God, Jesus Christ, the ministry of the Holy Spirit, prayer, the church, the Bible and Christian service. If you focus on these things with your time and energy then many of life's problems will fade away. You will not have time for the things of the earth if you focus on these priorities of God.

The role of knowledge in developing the mind

What help do we get in developing the mind and our thinking? One of the ways is putting into our minds the right information. Correct knowledge is information that can lead to correct thinking of the mind. The Bible has much to say about knowledge. A key verse is Hosea 4:6, which says, *My people are destroyed from a lack of knowledge.* (Hosea 4:6 NIV). Another translation says, *My people are destroyed for lack of knowledge* (KJV). No matter how Hosea 4:6 is translated, a lack of knowledge is detrimental to the Christian walk.

> I can stand what I know. It's what I don't know that frightens me.
> **—Frances Newton in: Draper p.367**

Ignorance and a lack of knowledge brings destruction and cancels victory for the Christian. God is a God of truth and he expects us to walk in the truth. Knowing the truth begins with correct information, that is, knowledge. The Bible speaks of the role of knowledge to both the Jews and the Christians. The Old Testament states,

- *The fear of the Lord is the beginning of knowledge, but fools despise wisdom and instruction.* Proverbs 1:7
- *For the Lord gives wisdom; from his mouth come knowledge and understanding* (Proverbs 2:6).
- *The wise store up knowledge, but the mouth of a fool invites ruin* (Proverbs 10:14).
- *The discerning heart seeks knowledge, but the mouth of a fool feeds on folly* (Proverbs 15:14).
- *Apply your heart to instruction and your ears to words of knowledge* (Proverbs 23:12).
- *Not only was the Teacher wise, but he also imparted knowledge to the people. He pondered and searched out and set in order many proverbs* (Ecclesiastes 12:9)
- *To these four young men God gave knowledge and understanding of all kinds of literature and learning* (Daniel 1:17)

These Old Testament verses tell us that wisdom, knowledge and instruction are important and they lead us to a relationship with

God. Knowledge can be stored up in our brains. God can give us knowledge beyond our circumstance. Finally, the knowledge that we receive should be passed onto others. In Ecclesiastes 12:9, the Teacher imparted his knowledge to the people.

The New Testament has its own perspective on knowledge. The following verses give insight and examples of knowledge. Highlighted are knowledge of God, the truth, Jesus Christ and the Scripture.

- *Meanwhile a Jew named Apollos, a native of Alexandria, came to Ephesus. He was a learned man, with a thorough knowledge of the Scriptures* (Acts 18:24).
- *So that you may live a life worthy of the Lord and please him in every way: bearing fruit in every good work, growing in the knowledge of God* (Colossians 1:10).
- *Paul, a servant of God and an apostle of Jesus Christ to further the faith of God's elect and their knowledge of the truth that leads to godliness* (Titus 1:1).
- *But grow in the grace and knowledge of our Lord and Saviour Jesus Christ. To him be glory both now and forever! Amen* (2 Peter 3:18).

Biblical knowledge is foundational to success in the Christian life. Knowledge of Scripture leads to a better relationship with Jesus Christ. It leads to a clearer understanding of who God is and who Jesus is. This is pleasing to the Lord. Scholars would agree that knowledge alone is only a beginning of Christian development. The knowledge that we gain should be used to serve God and people. Without actions, our knowledge is only cold orthodoxy and can lead to pride.

> He who knows everything has a lot to learn.
> **—Draper p.507**

Dr. Benjamin Bloom

The renowned American educator Dr. Benjamin Bloom has given us a way of understanding the educational process that guides us in presenting someone mature in Christ. Dr. Bloom presents an educational method that we can apply to the Christian perspective.

Before Benjamin Bloom educators often looked at teaching as one dimensional. That is, that knowledge is the main component of education. After Benjamin Bloom, teachers began to focus on three aspects of education so as to present a more complete philosophy of education. These three components, called "domains," are the cognitive domain (mental skills), the affect domain (feelings, emotions, attitudes), and the psychomotor domain (skills). The three components, as suggested by Dr. Bloom, will be examined in the chapters 4, 5 and 6. The three domains look like this:

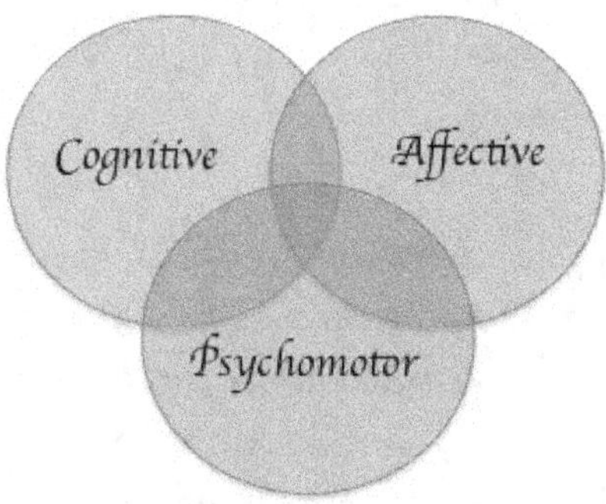

A simpler way of expressing the relationship between the three domains is:

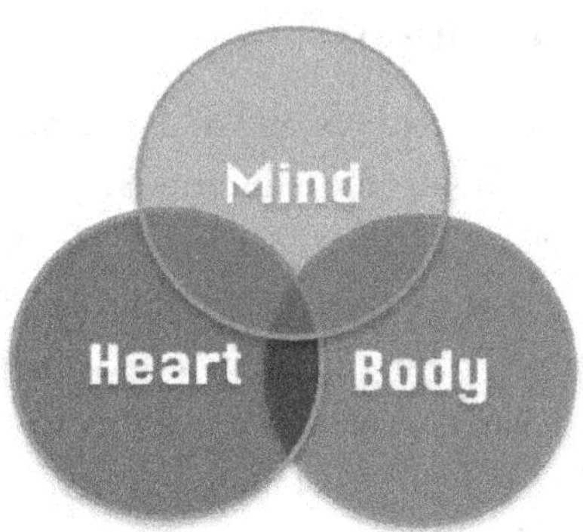

A third way of expressing the relationship is head, heart, and hands.

> Bloom's Taxonomy was created in 1956 under the leadership of educational psychologist Dr. Benjamin Bloom in order to promote higher forms of thinking in education, such as analyzing and evaluating concepts, processes, procedures, and principles, rather than just remembering facts (rote learning). It is most often used when designing educational, training, and learning processes.
>
> —http://www.nwlink.com

Bloom was responsible for broadening our understanding of education in a holistic manner. Bloom's focus on the development of the mind is called "Cognitive Development." A thorough study of Bloom is not needed here and has been covered by many, both in books and on the Internet. However, the importance of Bloom's work can be summarised.

> This domain focuses on intellectual skills and is familiar to educators. Bloom's Taxonomy is frequently used to describe the increasing complexity of cognitive skills as students move from beginner to more advanced in the knowledge of content. The cognitive domain is the core learning domain. The other

domains (affective and psychomotor require at least some cognitive component.

—http://pixel.fhda.edu

Bloom's method

To improve a student's ability to think, a teacher should study Benjamin Bloom's "taxonomy of cognitive development." Bloom helps students move from the simple to the complex levels of thinking (cognition). In a brief-summary fashion, the six levels of Bloom's cognitive development are:

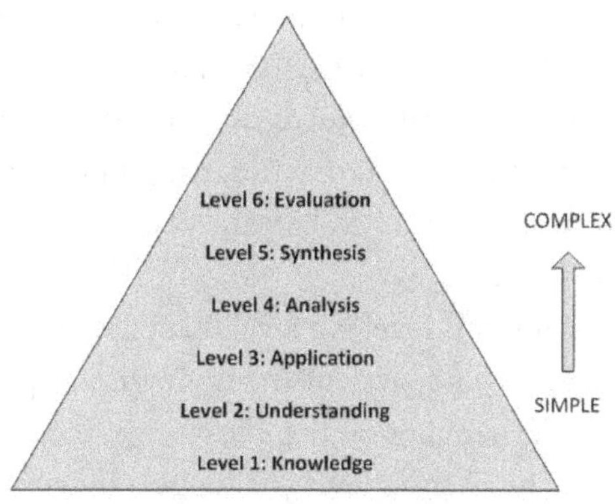

Bloom's Taxonomy: Levels 1 - 6

Level 1: The Knowledge level is defined as recalling previously learned facts or information and lays a foundation for all the other levels of cognitive development. The knowledge level is the entry level of education and is especially useful for beginning students or subjects. Similar words are recall, memorize, arrange, repeat and restate. Rote learning is on this level. A teacher on this level says, "Here are the facts you need to learn and know."

Level 2: The Comprehension level is the basic level of a student understanding the material being taught. The comprehension level builds on the knowledge level and takes a student deeper into understanding the material being presented by the teacher. Similar words used to describe the comprehension level are understand, repeat, restate, recognize, report and explain. A teacher on the comprehension level says, "Do you understand the material being taught today?"

Level 3: The Application level is familiar to every preacher of God's word. Application deals more with doing than knowing. The application level builds on the knowledge and comprehension levels. The application level is concerned with what a student will do with the information being presented. It is an action-oriented level. Without the application level, the information stays in student's head and does not affect his or her life. Similar words used to describe the application level are demonstrate, interpret, practice, use and illustrate. A teacher on the application level says, "What are you going to do with the material presented today?"

Level 4: The Analysis level is a level that takes a subject apart and examines it. A teacher and student break down a topic into smaller parts. The analysis level builds on the knowledge, comprehension and application levels. The analysis level challenges students to examine in detail the parts that make up the whole of a topic. Similar words for this level are examine, dissect, divide, experiment, question and appraise. After analysis of pastoral counselling skills and problems a teacher on this level says, "Let us examine and discuss the problem of why pastors need better counselling-skills and training."

Level 5: The Synthesis level is a level that puts things back together. Level 5 grows out of Level 4. They work together. After analysis has taken place (Level 4), then Level 5 can operate. Teachers and students need to put the parts of the discussion together again to form a solution. This level encourages thinking on a high level, as it is a level of problem solving. Helpful words in understanding this level are assemble, construct, create, design, organize and solve. A teacher on this level says, "What is the solution to the problem of a lack of pastoral training in counselling?" This level asks students to come up with answers to problems that are raised by the teacher.

Level 6: The Evaluation level is a level that tests or evaluates student conclusions to problems raised in class. The evaluation level builds on all the previous five levels. This level encourages students to test the theories or solutions to problems raised by the teacher or the context of ministry. According to Bloom, it is the highest level of cognitive development. Similar words to describe this level are test, evaluate, discover and appraise. A teacher on this level asks, "What are the strengths and weaknesses of the proposed plan of action?"

Dr. Benjamin Bloom is worth studying in greater detail than can be presented here. For further resources on Bloom's cognitive development see;

http://cehdclass.gmu.edu/ndabbagh/Resources/IDKB/bloomstax.htm

The intellect plays a key role in Christian maturity. Teachers are most familiar with the cognitive (mind) as one cannot teach without giving a minimum amount of content, information or data. Adult cognitive development is the study presented in this chapter and seeks a vision for teaching adults and helping them to mature.

Teaching for Cognitive Development

How did Jesus teach for cognitive development? I see several methods that Jesus used to develop properly the Cognitive in the disciples. He both taught correct information and secondly, he asked probing questions. One of the things Jesus did was to give correct information. The masses had been taught many ideas but those ideas were from men and not from God. Jesus corrected false teaching with true teaching. He challenged the assumptions of his day. He also spoke with authority.

The Sermon on the Mount is where Jesus gave a lot of true information and application to the lives of the listeners. A good summary of his teaching information in the Sermon on the Mount. In list form, from Matthew 5-7 the content would be;

- The Beatitudes,
- Salt and Light,
- Jesus fulfilled the Law,
- Anger and Murder,
- Lust and Adultery,
- Divorce and Remarriage,
- Oaths,
- Love Your Enemies,
- Giving to the Needy,
- How to Pray,
- How to Fast,
- Treasures in Heaven,
- Do not Worry,
- Do not Judge,
- Ask, Seek, Knock,
- The Narrow Gate,
- False Prophets,
- The Wise Builder.

Second, Jesus asked probing questions. For example, he asked:

- *Can any of you by worrying add a single moment to your lifespan?* (Matthew 6:27).
- *Why are you anxious about clothes?* (Matthew 6:28).
- *Why do you harbour evil thoughts?* (Matthew 9:4).
- *To what shall I compare this generation?* (Matthew 11:6).
- *And why do you break the commandments of God for the sake of your tradition?* (Matthew 15:3).
- *Who do people say the Son of Man is?* (Matthew 16:13).
- *But who do you say that I am?* (Matthew 16:15).
- *What profit would there be for one to gain the whole world and forfeit his life and what can one give in exchange for his life?* (Matthew 16:26).

Jesus presented his teachings in accordance with the style of teachers in his day. A teacher would gather students around himself and begin to teach them in a small group. Note Matthew 5:1,

> *Now when Jesus saw the crowds, he went up on a mountainside and sat down. His disciples came to him, and he began to teach them.*

Also, the New Testament records that; *Jesus went throughout Galilee, teaching in their synagogues, proclaiming the good news of the kingdom* (Matthew 4:23). He instructed the disciples as they travelled along the road of life. *After Jesus had finished instructing his twelve disciples, he went on from there to teach and reach in the towns of Galilee* (Matthew 11:1).

Teaching for cognitive growth today

There are similarities and differences between the time of Jesus and today. The content of our teaching remains the same but the delivery method is different. The truths that Jesus taught are timeless and echo throughout all time. Nevertheless, the way we teach today is different than it was in Jesus day. As pointed out above, a teacher would gather a group of students around himself and then teach them. There was no formal schooling with certificates, school fees and classroom lectures. Today we follow the formal schooling model. Therefore, we have to ask ourselves, how can we improve our teaching in regards to helping students to think (cognition)? Rather than rely on rote memory of our teachings, can teachers help students to become problem solvers?

> The mediocre teacher tells. The good teacher explains. The superior teacher demonstrates. The great teacher inspires.
> —**Ward https://www.brainyquote.com**

Two types of courses to teach

In teaching for cognitive development, I see two types of classes. The first class is a more straightforward lecture where a student does not have a lot of background in the subject. A student comes to class with little experience in the topic that the teacher will present. Classes in this type of teaching would be biblical languages, research methods and the more complex theological courses.

The second type of class would be classes that students have some background in. These would include courses in preaching, discipleship, evangelism, English and a host of other courses that a students would have some pre-class experience and information about. The following suggestions are for improving our teaching and helping students to think.

General recommendations

First, to encourage cognitive development, the teacher should be spiritually and academically prepared for every class. Otherwise, he or she is speaking in the flesh and not in the Spirit. To be prepared means to be familiar with the topic under study and have a passion for the material.

Second, the teacher should know the students and help them to be the best learners they can be. This is the Jesus model of teaching. In some colleges, this is difficult due to large class size. However, a teacher should strive to get to know as many students as he or she can.

Third, the teacher should ensure that the classroom is conducive for learning. This includes making sure there is chalk, lights, books, papers, Bibles and writing materials for the students. In some colleges this is difficult due to a lack of finances. Nevertheless, a teacher should make some simple sacrifices to help students learn.

Some specifics

How to teach for cognitive development?

- A teacher needs to challenge students to think on a higher level. This comes through Bloom's six levels of cognitive development.

- Second, since it is the intellectual level that is being discussed, a teacher needs to prepare quality notes and handouts for every class. As part of the notes the teacher needs to have a clear outline and goal for each particular class. He or she can add some scholarly quotes for discussion sake. The notes serve as a reminder of the lesson.

- Using visuals in the 21st century for intellectual development is important. This means computer usage, Power Point and a video projector.

- A teacher can use challenging questions for discussion to improve student thinking.

- Guided research papers also give good intellectual challenges for students.

- Case studies for discussion are also helpful in generating classroom discussion.

Conclusion

The goal of all these suggestions is an improvement in teaching for student thinking and problem solving. A student who graduates and enters the work world needs to have problem solving skills as they will have to face a world full of problems and people will look to school graduates as problem solvers. These skills begin with the development of the mind, correct knowledge and problem solving skills. The mind is the foundation for this process.

Study Questions

1. Why is the study of the mind important for students?
2. Briefly summarise Bloom's six levels of cognitive development.
3. How can you help students be better problem solvers?

CHAPTER 6

THE HEART IN TEACHING

Teachers are responsible for the internal qualities of student development. This can come in a variety of ways in our teaching but they come mainly through the love and care for our students. For example, Senka Hadzimuratovic told the following story:

Case study #10

I moved to the United States to a town that had very few immigrants. I spoke no English but had a passion for the language. My teacher saw this in me. After two years in the country, I spoke and wrote fairly well. But it was my teacher who helped me truly begin to conquer the language. Even though the teacher had 30 students in the class she took the time to help me with English. She rewarded me for my efforts with the language. My teacher cared for me and probably didn't know at the time that she had sparked my higher interests in education and my career. Now I have a journalism degree and a good job in communications and public relations.

—Senka Hadzimuratovic in https://www.buzzfeed.com

In the previous chapter, we talked about the head, heart, and hands working together in Christian maturity. This chapter will focus on developing the heart as part of Christian education.

Unger's Bible Dictionary describes the heart as:

1.   The centre of the bodily life (Psalm 40:8).

2.   The centre of the rational-spiritual nature of man (Romans 6:17).

3.   The centre of moral life (Psalm 73:26).
      The heart is the centre of the entire man, the very heart of life's impulse (Unger p.462).

We talk about a person who has a heart for the Lord. Pastors often have a heart for the people in their congregation. Missionaries have a heart for the unsaved. The Bible speaks of the heart as the centre of our emotions. The heart leads to commitment and conviction because we feel passionate about a truth that has been formulated and articulated in the cognitive domain.

Dr. Bloom, Part 2 The "Affect"
(emotion, heart)

We continue with our study of Dr. Ben Bloom's vision for teaching for personal growth. We explored the mind, knowledge and cognition in the last chapter. In this chapter, we will study Bloom's second category of growth, which he calls the "affect." The affect, or affective domain, "includes the manner in which we deal with things emotionally, such as feelings, values, appreciation, enthusiasms, motivations and attitudes."

(http://www.nwlink.com/~donclark/hrd/Bloom/ affective_domain.html).

You can see that the affect relates to the inner person and their emotions and heart. To the Christian this relates to the development of the inner spiritual life. This will be explored in this chapter.

Understanding "affect"

Several scholarly articles will be consulted to help us understand what Bloom means by "affect."

> In the educational literature, nearly every author introduces their paper by stating that the affective domain is essential for learning but it is the least studied, most often overlooked, the most nebulous and the hardest to evaluate of Bloom's three domains. There is significant value in realizing the potential to increase student learning by tapping into the affective domain. Affective topics in educational literature include attitudes, motivation, communication styles, classroom management styles, learning styles, use of technology in the classroom and nonverbal communication.
>
> —https://serc.carleton.edu/NAGTWorkshops/affective/
> intro.html

A second article says this about the affective domain:

> The affective domain is critical for learning but is often not specifically addressed. This is the domain that deals with attitudes, motivation, willingness to participate, valuing what is being earned, and ultimately incorporating the values of a discipline into a way of life.
>
> —http://pixel.fhda.edu/id/learning_domain.html

A third article says,

> The affective describes learning objectives that emphasize a feeling tone, as emotion, or a degree of acceptance or rejection. We found a large number of such objectives in the literature expressed as interests, attitudes, appreciations, values, and emotional sets or biases.
>
> —https://serc.carleton.edu/NAGTWorkshops/affective/
> intro.html

To this writer, the Affective Domain plays a key role in the maturing of Christians. The Christian life is more than an intellectual experience. It is a heart experience where our actions and behaviours match what we say we believe in our minds. It is being honest with ourselves and God, and living in a non-hypocritical way. This is all done in the power of the Holy Spirit as he leads us and teaches us and convicts us of all things. The Affective Domain speaks about developing the heart.

Bloom teaches that there are five stages of learning in the affective domain. They are;

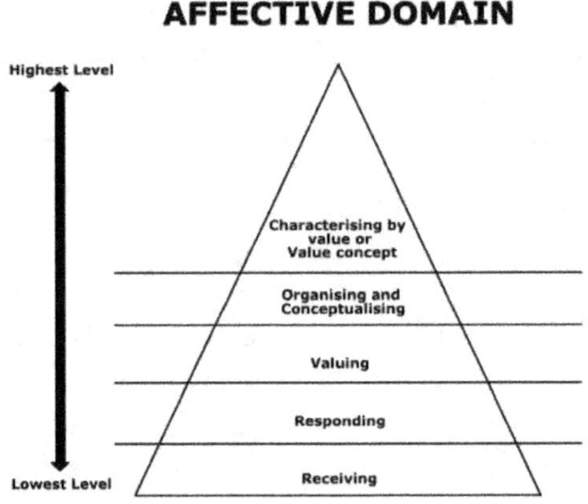

AFFECTIVE DOMAIN

- **Level 1 is Receiving:** (Willing to listen and receive). This means having open ears to the message of the Bible. Jesus said, *Whoever has ears to hear, let them hear.* (Mark 4:9). The Bible records the story of the Ethiopian official who met Philip and asked for help in understanding where he was reading in the Book of Isaiah. So Philip began to tell him the good news about Jesus. The man was willing to listen, receive Jesus, and be baptized. (Acts 8:26-39). His life changed forever from the inside out. Key words for understanding Level 1 are "hear, listen, look and be aware."

A person needs to move from Level 1 to Level 2 as they grow and mature.

- **Level 2 is Responding:** (Willingness to participate or respond). This means being desirous of making a change from within. God touched the Philippian jailer when Paul and Silas were in prison. The jailer said, *What must I do to be saved?* (Acts 16:30). Key words for understanding Level 2 are "participate, volunteer, follow and obey." A person needs to mature and move from Level 2 to Level 3.

- **Level 3 is Valuing:** (Acceptance of values). This means accepting a standard of behaviour, in our case, those standards of the Bible. The Pharisees valued behaviour with their minds but not their hearts. Jesus rebuked them for that.

> *Jesus said to the crowds and to his disciples: The Pharisees and the teachers of the Law are experts in the Law of Moses. So obey everything they teach you, but don't do as they do. After all, they say one thing and do something else.*
>
> —Matthew 23:1-3

Key words for understanding Level 3 are "act, express and display." A person needs to move to Level 4.

- **Level 4 is Organizing:** (Organizing a value system). This means being consistent in your overall lifestyle and a commitment to a set of values. Right choices are needed for this Level. Peter writes,

> *For this very reason, make every effort to add to your faith goodness; and to goodness, knowledge; and to knowledge, self-control; and to self-control, perseverance; and to perseverance, godliness; and to godliness, mutual affection; and to mutual affection, love.*
>
> —2 Peter 1:5-7

Key words for this level are "decide, select, and balance." A person needs to move to a higher level of emotional maturity.

- **Level 5 is Characterization:** (Willingness to change one's behaviour or lifestyle). This means to actually make a change from within that affects one's way of living. People on this level have a lifestyle that is consistent with their value system. Cornelius, in Acts Chapter 10, was committed to Jewish traditions. However, God spoke to him through a vision to accept Gentiles into fellowship with the Jewish believers. Later Peter said, *But Goɨ has shown me that I must not call any person common or unclean* (Acts 10:28). Peter matured emotionally in his acceptance of the Gentiles into the church. Paul's words to the Galatian Christians illustrates this as well. *But the fruit of the Spirit is love, joy, peace, forbearance, kinɨness, gooɨness, faithfulness, gentleness anɨ self-control.* (Galatians 5:22-23). The first three: love, joy and peace are inner unseen qualities of the affective. Love, joy and peace should manifest themselves in observable characteristics like forbearance, kindness, goodness, faithfulness, gentleness, and self-control. Love, joy, and peace have to demonstrate themselves in the other characteristics. Key words for this level are "display, exhibit, internalize."

What is the value of the affective domain for the Christian teacher and student? In the Book of James, he writes, *Do not merely listen to the worɨ, anɨ so ɨeceive yourselves. Do what it says* (James 1:22). The Christian life is more than knowing in our heads: it is responding with our hearts and honest actions with our lives. The decisions we make are internal decisions that often are triggered by our emotions. Teachers need to help students to know and accept a new set of values especially if they are unfamiliar with biblical precepts for success in the Christian life.

New Understanding of Affect

Bloom was concerned about the development of the inner self and values. I have strayed from the classic definition of Bloom's "affect" and put it in the category of the Spirit and spiritual growth. That is, the development of the inner self or the spirit. In Christian terms, that means development of the spiritual side of the Christian life.

> Spirituality really means "Holy Spirit at work."
>
> **—Suenens in Draper p.586**

The next section of this book deals with the development of the inner spirit.

The Bible on Spiritual Growth

The Christian life has many goals. For example;

- **The glory of God.** *So whether you eat or drink or whatever you do, do it all for the glory of God* (1 Corinthians 10:31).
- **Discipleship.** *Therefore go and make disciples of all nations, baptizing them in the name of the Father and of the Son and of the Holy Spirit* (Matthew 28:19).
- **Ministry works.** *For we are God's handiwork, created in Christ Jesus to do good works, which God prepared in advance for us to do* (Ephesians 2:10).

One of the main goals of the Christian life is personal spiritual growth, maturity and development.

What is spiritual growth

Spiritual growth is the process of becoming more and more like Jesus Christ in our attitudes and actions. In terms of our attitudes, our goal is an internal change that conforms to the image of God. Our focus also becomes less about us and more about the Glory of God.

As far as actions are concerned, do our lives reflect the life of Christ in us? Does the way in which we live reflect that we are growing in Christ? Paul told the Ephesians, *For we are God's handiwork, created in Christ Jesus to do good works, which God prepared in advance for us to do* (Ephesians 2:10).

Spiritual growth is an inner work of the Holy Spirit that manifests itself with outward actions. Paul said, *Therefore, if anyone is in Christ, the new creation has come; The old has gone, the new is here!* (2 Corinthians 5:17).

> Spirituality describes the quest for God.
> **—Richard Peace in Baker p.658**

Peter was concerned about the inner life, the "affect" stating,

> *For this very reason, make every effort to add to your faith goodness; and to goodness knowledge; and to knowledge self-control; and to self-control, perseverance; and to perseverance, godliness; and to godliness, mutual affection; and to mutual affection, love. For if you possess these qualities in increasing measure, they will keep you from being ineffective and unproductive in your knowledge of our Lord Jesus Christ.*
>
> —2 Peter 1:5-8

The cognitive lays a foundation for the affect to function. The cognitive gives the proper information for the affect (the inner life) to function properly. Spiritual growth is a combination of right beliefs and right actions from the heart and is based on the truths of Scripture. The goal is to be like Christ. Philippians 2:5-8 teaches,

> *In your relationships with one another, have the same mindset as Christ Jesus: Who, being in very nature God, did not consider equality with God something to be used to his own advantage; rather, he made himself nothing by taking the very nature of a servant being made in human likeness, and being found in appearance as a man, he humbled himself by becoming obedient to death-even death on a cross!*

Being like Christ is mental, emotional and physical. That is both internal in the mind-set we have about ourselves and external in our willingness to serve others and not ourselves.

What is spiritual maturity?

Maturity, for the Christian, is a mental attitude based on years of walking with the Lord and experiencing him in day-to-day encounters with issues and problems that people face. It means looking at life from God's perspective. It means following God's priorities. Spiritual growth is for the young or new Christians and maturity is for older people who have experienced life's problems and blessings. Although a young Christian can have wisdom beyond their years, the mature are usually older people.

Maturity is not a onetime instantaneous experience but is born out over a lifetime of living and ministering for the Lord. The Bible has many verses related to maturity. For example;

- Colossians 1:28 *He is the one we proclaim, admonishing and teaching everyone with all wisdom, so that we may present everyone fully mature in Christ.* This verse is a good verse for visionary teachers. The goal is complete maturity, not in the world, not in business, not in science but in Christ Jesus. The teachers path to this completeness is "proclaiming" (declaring, announcing, stating, making known, broadcasting) and "admonishing" (advising, recommending, counselling, urging, exhorting) using wisdom which comes from the Holy Spirit and experience, to present students mature in their walk and relationship with Christ.

- Hebrews 5:14 *But solid food is for the mature, who by constant use have trained themselves to distinguish good from evil.* The writer to the Book of Hebrews states that solid food (teaching and the content of the teaching) will help students in two ways. First, once they reach a level of maturity they can feed themselves and do not need to rely on teachers. That is, they are self-feeders who can study the word of God for themselves and come up with the right conclusions about a particular passage. Second, the mature self-feeding Christian will be able to know the difference between good and evil. Culture sometimes gives a different view of good and evil and the mature believer will follow the leading of the Holy Spirit and the Scriptures.

- Ephesians 4:13 says,

> *Until we all reach unity in the faith and in the knowledge of the Son of God and become mature, attaining to the whole measure of the fullness of Christ.*

There are certain marks of mature believers that teachers need to encourage in their students. First, they live in harmony with each other and carry one another's burdens. Believers are to act as if they are actually from the same family, that is, brothers and sisters. Second, a mark of a mature believer is reaching a level of knowledge about Jesus Christ. Internal and external teachings are to be done if Christians are to reach a good level of maturity.

Developing the inner life

The "affect" is concerned about the development of inner attitudes and values. Ultimately, this is a spiritual activity because change comes from within, often based on information that is taught by a teacher. Several verses reinforce this idea. For example;

- Ephesians 3:16 *I pray that out of his glorious riches he may strengthen you with power through his Spirit in your inner being.* Several points for the teacher need to be made here. First, God is the one who develops the inner life, that is, the inner being. It is by God's grace and his glorious riches that our inner self is encouraged and developed. Second, the Spirit is the way in which God develops the inner life of the Christian. A proverb says, "All sunshine makes for a desert." In the same way, not all knowledge makes for true inner growth. A visionary teacher can encourage inner development but it is the Spirit of God, who by the grace of God develops the inner soul of the believer.

> After all, it is those who have a deep and real inner life who are best able to deal with the irritating details of the outer life.
> **—Evelyn Underhill in *Brainy Quotes***

- 2 Corinthians 4:16 *Therefore we do not lose heart. Though outwardly we are wasting away, yet inwardly we are being renewed day by day.* Even though our bodies are slowly dying, our inner spirit can grow and develop until the day we are called home by the Lord. We have hope as long as the inner life is growing and is experiencing renewing every day.

- 1 Peter 3:4 *Rather, it should be that of our inner self, the unfading beauty of a gentle and quiet spirit, which is of great worth in God's sight.*

  One of the marks of a successful development of the inner self is a humble quiet outlook on life. This ensures that God gets the glory from our lives and teaching. God honours the man or woman who lives accordingly. A strong inner humility is of great value to God.

General recommendations

First, in general, the basic recommendations for "affect" are the same as for cognitive. To encourage "affect" the teacher should be spiritually and academically prepared for every class. Otherwise, he or she is speaking in the flesh and not in the Spirit. To be prepared means to be familiar with the topic under study and have a passion for the material.

Second, the teacher should know the students and help them to be the best learners they can be. This is the Jesus model of teaching. In some colleges this is difficult due to large class size. Nevertheless, a teacher should strive to get to know as many students as he can on a personal level.

Third, the teacher needs to ensure that the classroom is conducive for learning. This includes making sure there is chalk, lights, books, papers, Bibles and writing materials for the students. In some colleges, this is difficult due to a lack of finances. Nevertheless, a teacher should make some simple sacrifices to help students learn.

Some specifics

How to teach for affect: that is, inner values, attitudes and spiritual growth. A teacher needs to:

First, role model the inner spiritual life. This can come invisibly by a teacher's attitude and general spiritual approach to the class. Determine what you want students to become and then be that person to them.

If you want them to value something then role model that thing in front of them. For example, *Be kind and compassionate to one another, forgiving each other, just as in Christ, God forgave you* (Ephesians 4:32). Also, *Follow my example, as I follow the example of Christ* (1Corinthians 11:1). Students learn a lot from what we are inside and are willing to follow that example of humility.

Second, rely on the Holy Spirit. This is important because the real teacher of inner spiritual values and change is the Holy Spirit. Jesus said,

> *...but the Advocate, the Holy Spirit, whom the Father will send in my name, will teach you all things and will remind you of everything I have said to you.*
>
> —John 14:26

The Holy Spirit not only teaches but he convicts of sin. This is the inner work of the Holy Spirit. Also; *When he comes, he will prove the world to be in the wrong about sin and righteousness and judgment* (John 16:8). The Holy Spirit works from the inside out. Rely on him for spiritual power in the classroom.

Third, to further develop the inner life, be with Jesus, that is, spend time with Jesus. The disciples were seen as being powerful in their message as they had been seen with Jesus.

> *When they saw the courage of Peter and John and realized that they were unschooled, ordinary men, they were astonished and they took note that these men had been with Jesus.*
>
> —Acts 4:13

Nothing is more powerful for the classroom than a teacher who has spent time with Jesus. This can be in the form of prayer, study, and mediation on the word of God, especially those passages where Jesus speaks, teaches, and performs miracles.

Results of inner life development

When we encourage the inner life, we are encouraging students to have a closer walk with God. This will benefit the student as well as their family and the church as a whole. A good goal to aim for is the fruit of the Spirit. Paul told the Galatian Christians, *But the fruit of the Spirit is love, joy, peace, forbearance, kin◆ness, goo◆ness, faithfulness, gentleness an◆ self-control. Against such things there is no law* (Galatians 5:22-23). These are high goals and take more than one day to accomplish.

Conclusion

The development of the inner life is critical for the success of each Christian. God desires that we grow spiritually and this comes from the development of the inner spirit, values, and attitudes towards God, ourselves, our neighbours. God has given us teachers, the Holy Spirit, the Bible, and prayer to help us accomplish these high goals.

Study Questions

1. What is "affect?"
2. Why is the development of the inner life so important to the Christian?
3. What are some means for helping people to grow spiritually?

CHAPTER 7

THE PSYCHOMOTOR IN TEACHING

The commentator, Matthew Henry, wrote;

> If we heard a sermon every day of the week, and an angel from heaven was the preacher, yet, if we rested in hearing only, it would never bring us to heaven. Mere hearers are self-deceivers. And make this distinction, it is not for his deeds, that anyone is blessed, but in his deeds. It is not talking, but walking, that will bring us to heaven. Thus Christ will become more precious to the believer's soul.
>
> —http://biblehub.com/james/1-22.htm

What is Psychomotor (Bloom Part 3)

We continue with Bloom's taxonomy of learning with this important chapter on encouraging students to be doers and take action with what we are teaching them. As educators, we need to have a vision for the psychomotor. In simple terms, that means action. Our teaching needs to be combined with action otherwise our teaching can become only dull lectures.

What is psychomotor? Psychomotor is the development of skills in the students. For example, in a homiletics class it means students will demonstrate their ability in preaching. In a class on evangelism, it means students will show that they can present the gospel in an accurate and understandable way. In an Old Testament Survey class student will present papers on issues found in the Old Testament. These presentations will help students develop skills in research and classroom presentations; presentations which are then critiqued by his or her fellow students. This creates dialogue and thinking skills.

Assignments, which lead to doing, will tap into the abilities that students already have and help to speed up learning in its depth and impact. In a survey on leadership skills, I asked students how the seminary can better train leaders. In favour of the traditional approach, a small percentage of students identified workshops, teaching, and better materials as a part of the way to leadership skills. They identified courses or materials that would stimulate their thinking. However, the overwhelming majority identified ministry involvement as the path to leadership skills. Putting students into serious leadership roles was the major answer given for developing skills. The words participation, mentoring, small groups, ministry responsibilities and godly examples came up throughout their responses. We have the process reversed when we give a lot of academic teaching and only a small amount of opportunity for skills development.

Bloom Explained

There are several stages of development in Bloom's psychomotor domain. Many scholars have their own version of how many stages there are so I have selected this explanation of Bloom's approach to psychomotor. In picture form it would look like this;

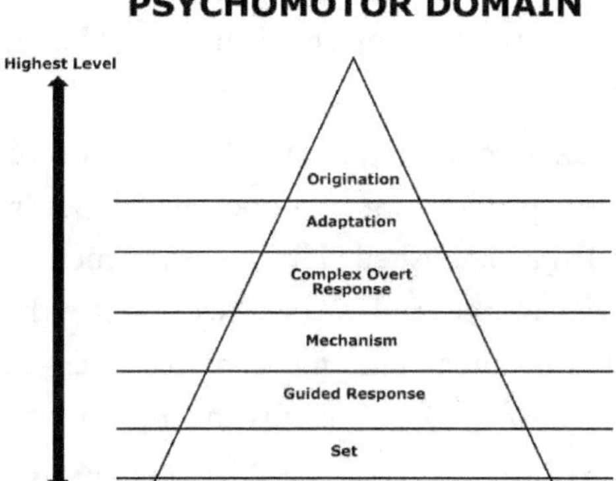

Each stage can be briefly described as follows:

- **Stage 1 Perception:** The ability to visualize the lesson in action. Key words to explain "perception" are describes, identifies and selects.
- **Stage 2 Set:** Readiness to act. It includes aspects of human personality such as mental, physical and emotional make up. It implies a minimum level of confidence in how to perform a task. Key words to explain "set" are moves, shows, states and displays.
- **Stage 3 Guided response:** The teacher steers the students in a particular direction. Imitation and trial and error are encouraged. Practicing is part of the "guided response." Key words to explain "guided response" are reproduce, copy, reproduce and follow. The key word is "guided" where the teacher guides the students in their development.
- **Stage 4 Mechanism:** This phase encourages students to become somewhat proficient in the development of skills through constant practice. It is not a beginning phase but an intermediate phase in the development of skills. The skills flow more easily out of the students as they learn and become more comfortable with the skills under

study. A minimum level of confidence is developed in the students. Key words in understanding "mechanism" would be displays, fixes, measures, mixes and organizes.

- **Stage 5 Complex overt response:** The complex relates to the skills development progressing to a good level. Complex physical functions (skills) are established. This level assumes a high level of skills development by the students as they practice the skill under study. Key words in understanding "complex overt response" are build, constructs, displays, fixes, mends and assembles.

- **Stage 6 Adaptation:** The level of development is such that a student can add his or her own interpretation of the skill under development. Key words in understanding "adaptation" would be adapts, alters, changes, reorganizes and re-creates.

- **Stage 7 Origination:** Students are encouraged to create original ideas in the development of new skills and patterns. The phase is the advanced mastery of skills. Learning emphasizes creativity and originality. Key words to explain "origination" would be rearrange, compose, construct, design and build. (With help for these categories from: https://en.wikipedia.org/wiki/Bloom %27s_taxonomy#The_psychomotor_domain_.28action-based.29).

Summary of Bloom's psychomotor domain

Rather than a written exam, the psychomotor is best tested in a face-to-face action-based evaluation. In learning new skills, a student can learn best by doing rather than just hearing. The psychomotor is an action domain and evaluations (grades) are based on performance more than written papers.

> The true object of education should be to train one to think clearly and to act rightly.
> **—McKenzie p.6**

A second aspect of psychomotor domain is a teacher himself doing more than reading his or her notes. A teacher can encourage classroom activities based on the lesson being taught. Action oriented teaching uses methods like debates, student presentations, role-play, demonstrations, using outside experts and much more.

The Bible on Skills Development

The Bible has much to say about psychomotor, that is, skills development. Christians are encouraged to grow spiritually and also make disciples, evangelize, teach, preach, encourage, pray, rebuke, correct, council, sacrifice, give, help and other skills which need to be taught and practiced before they are mastered. Some Christians are fast learners and some are slow learners. In the average classroom, a teacher can expect a few students to be excellent in skills development. Some to be good in skills development. Some to be average in skills development, and a few to be slower learners in developing skills. In a class on preaching, for example, some students are naturally gifted in public speaking, therefore they pick up skills in preaching rather quickly. Some lack confidence in public speaking and they need to be encouraged in their homiletical skills development. Preaching skills are learned by knowing what the skills are and then practicing those skills. Both knowing and doing are necessary for successful preaching.

Specific verses on action Christianity

Different people in the Bible have different things to say about doing Christianity not just thinking about Christianity. For example;

1. Jesus

Jesus was the master teacher who taught not only that men and women should know the truth but that they should do the truth. Jesus emphasized being obedient to his words. For example;

Luke 6:46 *Why do you call me, "Lord, Lord," and do not do what I say?* Jesus was concerned about more than a mental commitment to himself. He spoke of the need to let our actions show that we have learned what he said.

Second, Jesus emphasised doing the will of God more than merely knowing the will of God.

> *Not everyone who says to me, "Lord, Lord," will enter the kingdom*
> *of heaven, but only the one who does the will of my Father who is*
> *in heaven.*
>
> —Matthew 7:21

Action was important to Jesus. As the saying says, "actions speak louder than words."

Be like Jesus in your actions and not your appearance.
—Quoted in a sermon by Pastor Todd Patterson

Pastor Richard Beaton writes about Matthew 7:21 stating,

This is a powerful passage that gets at the heart of Jesus' message. To be a follower of Jesus means that behaviors and actions (the manner in which we live out our daily lives) are the artifacts of the inner life of faith.

—http://www.workingpreacher.org/preaching.aspx?
commentary_id=88

2. James

James, the half-brother of Jesus, had some equally powerful things to say about our actions which should match what we say with our mouths. For example, he said,

> *Do not merely listen to the word, and so deceive yourselves. Do what it says... Religion that God our Father accepts as pure and faultless is this: to look after orphans and widows in their distress and to keep oneself from being polluted by the world.*
>
> —James 1:22-27

James was committed to living a life of no hypocrisy where his actions did not match his words. James encouraged Christians to live the same way.

A second powerful teaching by James on being a person of action states,

> *What good is it, my brothers and sisters, if someone claims to have faith but has no deeds? Can such faith save them?.. In the same way, faith by itself, if it is not accompanied by action, is dead. But someone will say, "You have faith; I have deeds." Show me your faith without deeds, and I will show you my faith by my deeds. You foolish person, do you want evidence that faith without deeds is useless? You see that his (Abraham) faith and his actions were working together, and his faith was made complete by what he did. You see that a person is considered righteous by what they do and not by faith alone.*
>
> —James 2:14-26 edited

> People may doubt what you say, but they will always believe what you do.
>
> **—McKenzie p.4**

If James were here today preaching in your church he would say, "Be sure your actions equal your words, otherwise your Christianity is useless."

3. The Apostle Paul

Paul also has much to say about an action-oriented Christianity. Action, in this case, means love. Love manifests itself through action. Paul lays out what true love is in his letter to the Corinthians stating;

> *If I speak in the tongues of men or of angels, but do not have love, I am only a resounding gong or a clanging cymbal. If I have the gift of prophecy and can fathom all mysteries and all knowledge, and if I have a faith that can move mountains, but do not have love, I am nothing. If I give all I possess to the poor and give over my body to hardship that I may boast, but do not have love, I gain nothing.*
>
> *Love is patient, love is kind. It does not envy, it does not boast, it is not proud. It does not dishonour others, it is not self-seeking, it is not easily angered, it keeps no record of wrongs. Love does not delight in evil but rejoices with the truth. It always protects, always trusts, always hopes, always perseveres.*
>
> *—1 Corinthians 13:1-7*

To the Apostle Paul, love motivates action. We show love by what we do more than what we say. A husband may tell his wife he loves her, which is important, but the wife may believe his actions more than what he says. It is true that love is one of the most misused words in the English language. It should only be used when there is a commitment to back it up with deeds.

> Works, not words, are the proof of love.
> **—McKenzie p.7**

Paul says that being doers in the faith is for the praise and thanks to God who enables us to do good deeds.

> *And whatever you do, whether in word or deed, do it all in the name of the Lord Jesus, giving thanks to God the Father through him.*
> —Colossians 3:17

4. Luke

Luke gets in on the action stating,

> *Now the Berean Jews were of more noble character than those in Thessalonica, for they received the message with great eagerness and examined the Scriptures every day to see if what Paul said was true.*
> —Acts 17:11

To Luke, searching the Scriptures was a mark of integrity. This searching led to practicing and embracing what it says.

> Many people would rather study the Bible than practice what it teaches.
> **—McKenzie p.5**

5. John

Not to be left out, John states, *Dear children, do not let anyone lead you astray. The one who does what is right is righteous, just as he is righteous* (1 John 3:7). He also writes,

Dear friend, do not imitate what is evil but what is good. Anyone who does what is good is from God. Anyone who does what is evil has not seen God.

—3 John 11

John continues to reinforce the teaching that in education, knowing involves doing. Knowing is the beginning of education and doing is the end of education.

> Our words may hide our thoughts, but our actions will reveal them.
>
> **—McKenzie p.7**

In a lengthy quote, Pastor Rick Warren gives a clear understanding of the importance of doing in the Christian walk.

From Pastor Rick Warren

Receiving, reading, researching, remembering, and reflecting on the Word of God are all useless if we fail to put them into practice. We must become *doers of the word* (James 1:22).

I understand this is a hard step, because Satan fights it so intensely. He doesn't mind you going to Bible studies as long as you don't do anything with what you learn. We fool ourselves when we assume that just because we have heard or read or studied a truth, we have internalized it.

Actually, you can be so busy going to the next class or seminar or Bible conference that you have no time to implement what you've learned. You forget it on the way to your next study. Without implementation, all our Bible studies are worthless. Jesus said,

Everyone who hears these words of mine and puts them into practice is like a wise man who built his house on the Rock.

—Matthew 7:24 NIV

Jesus also pointed out that God's blessing comes from obeying the truth, not just knowing it. He said, *Now that you know these things, you will be blesse* if you *o them* (John 13:17).

I cannot overstate the value of being a part of a small Bible study discussion group. We always learn from others truths we would never learn on our own. Other people will help you see insights you would miss and help you apply God's truth in a practical way.

The best way to become a *oer of the Wor* is to always write out an action step as a result of your reading or studying or reflecting on God's Word. Develop the habit of writing down exactly what you intend to do.

This action step should be personal (involving you), practical (something you can do), and provable (with a deadline to do it). Every application will involve either your relationship to God, your relationship to others, or your personal character. Questions:

1. What has God already told you to do in his Word that you haven't started doing yet?
2. With whom are you sharing what you learn and apply from God's Word?

(http://pastorrick.com/devotional/english/become-a-doer-of-the-word).

General recommendations

Like with cognitive and affective development, to encourage psychomotor development the teacher should be spiritually and academically prepared for every class. Otherwise, he or she is speaking in the flesh and not in the Spirit. To be prepared means to be familiar with the topic under study and have a passion for the material through personal experience. You can only teach effectively what you have practiced consistently.

Second, the teacher should know the students and help them to be the best learners they can be. This is the Jesus model of teaching. In some colleges, this is difficult due to large class sizes. Nevertheless, a teacher should strive to get to know as many students as he can.

Third, the teacher should ensure that the classroom is conducive for learning. This includes making sure there is chalk, lights, books, papers, Bibles and writing materials for the students. In some colleges, this is difficult due to a lack of finances. Nevertheless, a teacher should make some simple sacrifices to help students learn.

Some specifics

The students should be put into action to help them develop skills in doing what the teacher is teaching. For example, in a homiletics class, students should preach more than one or two times. To do this they could form "preaching groups" to practice short sermons outside of class. In language classes, the students could be encouraged to teach what they learned to their fellow students. One saying says, "To teach is to learn twice." Action reinforces knowledge. Internships, where possible, could be encouraged for a period of time such as in planting a church, serving in a church, teaching a Sunday school class.

Teachers need to teach their classes using a variety of methods and not just lecture. An action-oriented class is better than a lecture oriented class. Teachers can encourage small group interactions and discussions, classroom student presentations, topical classroom discussions, debates and many more action oriented activities to stimulate doing.

Conclusion

The goal of all these items is an improvement in student learning though student activities that encourage doing as a way of learning. A student who graduates and enters the work world needs to have skills for ministry even before they arrive in a school, church or mission setting. Our teachers need to have a vision for doing as part of the learning process.

Study Questions

1. Why is encouraging "doing" so important in human development?
2. Briefly summarise Bloom's psychomotor domain.
3. What did Jesus have to say about doing?

LEARNING STYLES PART 1

Western

A good teacher has a vision for the importance of the students. This includes understanding both their background and how they learn. This learning aspect is officially called "Learning styles." Learning styles will take the next three chapters. Chapter 8 will look into learning styles as seen by Western writers. Chapter 9 will tackle African learning styles. Chapter 10 will examine the Bible on how we learn.

Learning styles seeks to understand how different students develop from different ways of learning. There is great overlap in learning styles. For example, most students learn from lectures, reading and taking notes. Nevertheless, there is room for individual differences between students. Every class is filled with a variety of student learning styles. For example, some students learn best by reading books. Some students learn best by hands-on activities such as practice preaching, teaching and evangelism. Some students learn best by themselves and some learn best in groups. When a teacher adds variety to his or her own teaching styles it helps more students who do not learn from the traditional lecture to be better learners.

> Every student can learn, just not on the same day or in the same way.
> —**George Evans in: http:// www.wiseoldsayings.com/learning- quotes/**

A student who is a good reader may not do well on practical assignments. In reverse, a student who is good in practical assignments may do poorly on a written exam. Neither student would be considered a poor student only that they learn in different ways. A teacher needs to add variety to his or her teaching style to include smart students who do well in one area but do not do well in other areas. A teacher can lecture and give quizzes and exams but should also include student presentations and actions (demonstrations) that include a wider variety of learning styles than simply writing down notes from a lecture and then taking a test.

Western Understanding of Learning Styles

Much study of learning styles has been done in the western context. This section will explore the styles as identified by Western education writers. These learning styles are not exclusive to western people as Africans and Westerners have similar learning style patterns. Nevertheless, I will speak in generalizations about Western learning styles.

In Christian circles, Mrs. Marlene LeFever has emerged as one of the main writers on learning styles. Her book, *Learning Styles: Reaching Everyone Go׳ Gave You to Teach* 1995, 2004 by Cook Communications Ministries, has been widely read in Christian circles.

The following learning styles will be studied in the following pages in this chapter;

1. The common sense learner "practical learner."
2. The analytical learner "the thinker learner."
3. The imaginative learner "the dreamer learner."
4. The dynamic learner "the go-getter learner."
5. The relational learner "the people learner."
6. The global learner "the big thinking learner."
7. The visual learner "the seerer learner."
8. The verbal (auditory) learner "the listener learner."
9. The kinaesthetic learner "the doer learner."

Not every student learns the same way. We need to understand, "that God has wired each brain differently" (Judith Lingenfelter p.69 in *Teaching Cross-Culturally*). The goal in this study is to better understand how students learn and how we can be more effective teachers by understanding student learning patterns or styles.

The Common Sense Learner

The common sense learner are to be found in every college. They are practical learners who stay away from philosophical discussions and do not like lectures with lots of notes and readings. They want to know how things work and like to take things apart and put them back together again. James, in the New Testament, is a good example of a common sense learner. He said, *Do not merely listen to the word, and so deceive yourselves. Do what it says* (James 1:22).

Common sense learners learn by doing and they would make a good practical theologian. They like small groups, are realistic and practical, excel in problem solving, learn through demonstrations, do not enjoy lectures and lots of note taking.

One problem with common sense learners is they do not like the theories and philosophy that often forms the foundation of our beliefs.

Doctrine plays an important part in laying the base for our practical ministries and should not be avoided by common sense learners.

How to teach common sense learners

- Prepare some handouts for each class. They learn better by what they read than by what they hear.
- Have students work in small groups and make a class presentation of their results.
- Send them out to interview people on the topic of the class. For example, if the class topic is on youth ministry, send the students out to talk to people doing youth ministry. Note that interviews and observations are most meaningful if the student knows ahead of time what they are trying to find out and observe. Interviews and observations should have a goal and should add to the student's knowledge and skills.
- Send them out to make visits and observations if the class topic is appropriate. If the class topic is on teaching Sunday school send the students out to visit churches and make observations on Sunday school teachers.
- Have some reflection papers. Get them to think about something they were doing and have them write a reflection paper on what they learned.

The Analytical Learner

The analytic learner learns best from organized lecturers when information is presented in an organized, systematic fashion. They like details, written documents, notes, information and outlines. They present well-planned papers that are neat and follow proper protocols. They love the traditional classroom where the teacher is the expert.

Although they find drama, debates and discussions entertaining, the real learning takes place when the teacher presents information in an organized and clear way.

The analytic learner makes for a good systematic theologian. Systematic theologians like to have doctrines and beliefs organized into neat categories with supporting documents as footnotes, endnotes and bibliographies.

Isaiah captures the analytic learner in Isaiah 28:9-10 (KJV);

> *Whom shall he teach knowledge? and whom shall he make to understand doctrine? them that are weaned from the milk, and drawn from the breasts. For precept must be upon precept, precept upon precept; line upon line, line upon line; here a little, and there a little.*

The Analytic Learner learns best from books, lectures, notes, teachers who are experts, theory, and make arguments defending their own position. They like to sit in the front of the class. They like ideas as much as they like people.

The Christians in Berea were more analytic than other places mentioned in the Book of Acts.

> *Now the Berean Jews were of more noble character than those in Thessalonica, for they received the message with great eagerness and examined the Scriptures every day to see if what Paul said was true.*
>
> —Acts 17:11

How to teach analytic learners

- Prepare a handout for each class.
- Have an additional suggested reading list for the topic at hand.
- Put some books on reserve to supplement the class notes.
- Prepare quality lectures.

- Have written assignments.
- Have students prepare a research paper.

Because of some problems with analytic learners, the teacher must be well prepared for possible questions from these learners. Analytic students may get distracted by the details, thus missing the big picture of what you are trying to teach. Analytic students may see themselves as elite or special students more advanced than other types of learners. Analytic students can get frustrated if the class moves too slowly for them as they pick up new ideas more quickly than other types of learners.

The Imaginative Learner

The imaginative learner is a dreamer who is in touch with their feelings. They like philosophy more than academics. They absorb ideas from teachers that the teacher may not have intended. They are good abstract thinkers and like to share ideas with others. They dream big dreams. An example in the Bible would be James and John, the two sons of Zebedee. For example;

> *Then James and John, the sons of Zebedee, came to him. "Teacher," they said, "we want you to do for us whatever we ask. What do you want me to do for you?" he asked. They replied, "Let one of us sit at your right and the other at your left in your glory."*
>
> —Mark 10:35-37

Imaginative learners ask "why" questions as they want to know about the bigger picture rather than fine details of a topic under discussion.

How to teach imaginative learners

- A teacher needs to ask philosophical questions in class.

- Teachers need to ask "why" questions such as "why do people behave the way they do?"
- Role play, situation games and dramas appeal to imaginative learners.
- Short reflective papers are good exercises for these students.
- Teachers can give adequate time for sharing ideas in small groups in class.

> Expecting all people to learn the same way is like expecting all people to wear the same size clothing.
> —**Madeline Hunter in: http://www.wiseoldsayings.com/**

Some problems with imaginative learners is that they dream in class and it appears to the teacher that they are not listening. They think philosophically and may have a hard time getting to the point of a topic or question. They do not like to argue and it may appear that they are uninterested in a topic under discussion. They think in bigger pictures, see all sides of an issue, and have a hard time coming up with one conclusion on a question. This may appear to the teacher as an inability to think and arrive at their position on a topic. They like to share their opinions with others and can appear as talkative in class to the teacher.

The Dynamic Learner

The dynamic learner has high energy, is energetic and outgoing. The dynamic learner has a vision and enthusiasm for life and is confident in God's leading in their life. They know where they are going in life and are excited about the journey to get to their goals. An example from the New Testament of a dynamic learner would be the Apostle Paul. He states,

> *Not that I have already obtained all this, or have already arrived at my goal, but I press on to take hold of that for which Christ Jesus took hold of me. Brothers and sisters, I do not consider myself yet to have taken hold of it. But one thing I do: Forgetting what is behind and straining toward what is ahead, I press on toward the goal to win the prize for which God has called me heavenward in Christ Jesus.*
>
> —Philippians 3:12-14

This passage shows that the Apostle Paul was a dynamic learner who had a vision for God and what God wanted him to do.

How to teach dynamic learners

- A teacher needs to be patient with dynamic learners as their level of energy and classroom performance is not like other students.
- A teacher needs to ask a lot of questions to keep the dynamic learner interested in the lesson at hand.
- Create action-oriented assignments where the students have to take a problem and discover solutions to the problem and then present their findings to the rest of the class.
- Dynamic students need to be sent out into the community to interview people on a variety of problems based on the subject of the class.

Some problems with dynamic learners is that they are hard to understand with their levels of energy. They jump in with an answer whenever a teacher asks a question. They take up a lot of class time with their questions. If a teacher makes small groups in class, the dynamic learner will assume leadership of the group from the start. This may appear as ego or pride to the teacher and fellow group members but it is their vision and energy at work.

The Relational Learner

What is relational learning? Relational learning is a way of learning whereby students and teachers learn from each other by sharing ideas and working together with those ideas. Relational learning is people based and people are the key to the learning process.

Relational learners learn from group situations where numbers of people are involved. They learn best from other people and are committed people-persons. They like human interactions and would rather be with people than with books. They like variety and can be easily bored with an academic lecture.

> God cares for people through people.
>
> **—McKenzie p.387**

The Apostle Paul encourages the Thessalonian Christians to be relational learners. He writes,

> *Now about your love for one another we do not need to write to you,*
> *for you yourselves have been taught by God to love each other.*
>
> —1 Thessalonians 4:9

The writer of the Book of Hebrews adds, *And let us consider how we may spur one another on toward love and good deeds* (Hebrews 10:24). The Bible has many other examples such as Jesus training of the 12 disciples as relational learners.

How to teach relational learners

- A teacher to relational learners needs to be warm towards the students and show that they care about the students.
- The teacher of relational learners needs to provide many group exercises such as small groups and study groups.
- People projects such as working with orphans and displaced persons provides good learning experiences for the students.
- Classroom presentations are a good learning tool for relational learners because they involve people in the learning task.

Some problems with relational learners are they are so people oriented that they may be late with assignments and term papers because they spent too much time with people and not enough time studying and preparing papers. They are sensitive to criticism and can become discouraged easily.

The Global Learner

The global learner is a "big picture" learner. He or she is challenged by big ideas and thoughts. The global learner likes to think in terms of major plans and ideas.

Jesus was an example of a global-thinking person. He said, *But seek first his kingdom and his righteousness, and all these things will be given to you as well* (Matthew 6:33). He also said,

> *Therefore go and make disciples of all nations, baptizing them in the name of the Father and of the Son and of the Holy Spirit, and teaching them to obey everything I have commanded you. And surely I am with you always, to the very end of the age.*
>
> —Matthew 28:19-20

Jesus taught on small things like fish, coins and sheep but never lost sight of the big picture: the glory of God, righteousness and the kingdom of God.

Global learners need to see purpose in their studies. How are their studies linked to a bigger task or purpose?

How to teach global learners

- A teacher to global learners should not get bogged down in the small details of any topic.
- The teacher should challenge the students with big ideas that are global and can bring major change to the world.
- The teacher can suggest projects that involve personal commitment to a big idea such as an evangelism programme or visiting a mission station.

Some problems with global learners are that they get bored and lose interest in a subject if the teacher focuses too much on details of any topic. Global learners lose interest in the topic if the teacher does not attach purpose to the lesson linking the lesson to a higher purpose than the lesson for that day.

The Visual Learner

The visual learner is just that, they learn by visualizing or seeing what you want them to learn. They may close their eyes to visualize the topic under discussion. They learn best by seeing. A visual learner would say, "Seeing is believing.

> Knowing it and seeing it are two different things.
>
> **—Suzanne Collins in: http://www.goodreads.com**

The Bible has several examples of visual learners. The writer of Proverbs 24:32 said, *I applied my heart to what I observed and learned a lesson from what I saw.* Seeing and applying to his life was important to the writer - who was probably King Solomon. In the New Testament, the Apostle Paul tells the Galatian Christians,

> *When I saw that they were not acting in line with the truth of the gospel, I said to Cephas in front of them all, "You are a Jew, yet you live like a Gentile and not like a Jew. How is it, then, that you force Gentiles to follow Jewish customs?*
>
> —Galatians 2:14

Paul learned from what he saw to correct the Christians in Galatia.

How to teach visual learners

- The successful teacher teaches visually with charts, graphs, handouts, pictures and maps.
- The visually minded teacher uses projectors, Power Point and Internet video clips.
- The visually minded student likes sometime between ideas presented by the teacher to visualize the topic more clearly.
- Provide for field trips to go and see what the subject for the day is talking about. If the lesson is on leadership go and visit some leaders in their work place and interview them.

Some problems with visual learners are a lack of materials in the classroom such as posters, pictures, charts, graphs, handouts, drawing materials and physical objects that can be handled. Another problem is a teacher who lacks creativity and does not use Power Point, digital displays and the use of computers and video projectors. Visual learners are visual in style and struggle with formal lectures. The teacher may misread the visual students thinking they are asleep when they are actually looking at the topic in their minds.

The Auditory Learner

An auditory learner learns best by listening. Auditory means relating to the sense of hearing. For a teacher who likes straight lectures, the auditory learning student is their favourite. Auditory learners like to sit in the front of the class so they can hear the teacher clearly.

The auditory student grasps ideas quickly as the teacher lectures. The auditory students likes instructions to be spoken clearly in relation to producing term papers and writing exams.

> God still speaks to those who take the time to listen.
>
> **—McKenzie p.309**

Mary, in the New Testament, is a good example of an auditory learner. Luke tells us, (Martha) *had a sister called Mary, who sat at the Lord's feet listening to what he said* (Luke 10:39). Mary was a good auditory learner.

How to teach auditory learners

- The teacher is to speak clearly and loudly for the auditory student.
- Provide oral exams and quizzes as well as written exams and quizzes.
- Give students the opportunity to present papers in class.

- Use small groups as they like interactions with other students.
- Ask questions in class using the question and answer technique of teaching.
- Give students the chance to re-teach the lesson to see how they comprehended the topic for the class.
- Have a clear introduction to the class and a summary at the end of the class.
- Use case studies where students have to come up with conclusions and make classroom presentation.

Some problems teaching auditory learners are they get discouraged easily if the teacher does not speak clearly and loudly. They are seen as teacher's pets because teachers like auditory students.

The Kinaesthetic Learner

Kinaesthetic learners learn best when there is physical movement involved in the learning task. For Bible College and seminary level teaching this usually means a "practicum" whereby the student goes out to do a project such as planting a church, working in a church, teaching in a primary or secondary school. The kinaesthetic learner is similar to the common sense learner but is more extreme. The kinaesthetic learner can also be referred to as a discovery learner. The discovery learner learns best by a hands on style of learning activities.

> Tell me and I forget. Teach me and I remember. Involve me and I learn.
> —**Benjamin Franklin. in: http://www.wiseoldsayings.com/learning-quotes/**

The writer in FamilyEducation.com says,

> Kinesthetic learners are most successful when totally engaged with the learning activity. They acquire information fastest when participating in a science lab, drama presentation, skit, field trip, dance, or other active activity.
>
> —http://school.familyeducation.com/intelligence/teaching-methods/38519.html#ixzz2nXuYql41

For the Bible College or seminary this means field trips and practicum exercises. The Bible has a few examples of kinaesthetic people. For example, *From the fruit of their lips people are filled with good things, and the work of their hands brings them reward* (Proverbs 12:14). From the New Testament,

> *Make it your ambition to lead a quiet life: You should mind your own business and work with your hands, just as we told you.*
>
> —1 Thessalonians 4:12

How to teach kinaesthetic learners

- Provide activities in the classroom such as drama, presentations and other hands on activities.
- Field trips can be useful with kinaesthetic learners.
- Practicum work is good for the kinaesthetic learner.

Some problems in teaching kinaesthetic learners are that they do not like the classroom very much. They do not learn much from lectures, note taking or exams. They sit near the door so they can move around during a lecture. They struggle with much that goes on in a traditional classroom.

Conclusion

It is important to remember that students are a mix of the learning styles presented in this chapter. They have a dominant learning style and then a secondary learning style. Teachers need to teach and provide something to all the styles in order to evaluate each student's performance. A teacher can lecture, use debates, have students' present papers and go out on a field trip depending on the class and topic under discussion. Variety is the key to meeting the needs of all the students. Therefore, a teacher needs to use lecture plus other learning activities to reach more student learning styles. The visionary teacher needs to be professional, creative, scholarly, practical, applicable, spiritual and aware of the learning styles of students in their classroom.

Study Questions

1. What do you think is your dominant learning style?
2. Which learning style is most common in Bible school or seminary students?
3. What learning style was Jesus?

CHAPTER 9

LEARNING STYLES PART 2

Africa

A good teacher has a vision for teaching using the strengths of the culture that he or she is teaching in. For West Africans that means paying attention to African Traditional Education (ATE).

The Nigerian educationist, Dr. Babs Fafunwa wrote his ground-breaking book *History of Education in Nigeria* which spelled out the more traditional Nigerian learning system. The Rev. Bitrus Thaba writes, "Dr. Babs Fafunwa, in his scholarly book, *History of Education in Nigeria*, asserts that Africans best learn through observation, imitation, and participation" (Janvier and Thaba 1993 p.58). This system is actually more biblical than the Western emphasis on academics and the formal schooling system. Thaba highlights the teaching-learning process as written by Dr. Fafunwa. Thaba goes onto say,

> However, adoption of Western approach to education has long changed that story and practice. Encyclopedia Americana confirms that, "The contemporary forms of education in African nations reflects the European concepts of education around which the systems developed before independence."
>
> —p.298

This chapter will examine the importance of the Nigerian system of learning based on Dr. Fafunwa's observation, imitation and participation formula for African learning styles.

Observation

Observational learning skills are taught from a very early age whereby the child observes the mother and father and learns by their behaviour in both what they say and what they do. This is called observational learning. How does observational learning work?

> Observational learning is learning that occurs through observing the behavior of others. It is a form of social learning which takes various forms, based on various processes. In humans, this form of learning requires a social model such as a parent, sibling, friend, or teacher. Particularly in childhood, a model is someone of authority or higher status.
> —https://en.wikipedia.org/wiki/Observational_learning

The writer Isabella Dugand writes,

> Observational learning describes the process of learning through watching others, retaining the information, and then later replicating the behaviors that were observed. Observational learning can be a powerful learning tool. When we think about the concept of learning, we often talk about direct instruction or methods that rely on reinforcement and punishment. But a great deal of learning takes place much more subtly and relies on watching the people around us and modeling their actions.
> —https://prezi.com/sub3gu0sd8hl/observational-learning/

> Observation, more than books and experience, are the prime educators.
>
> **—Amos Bronson in: https:// www.brainyquotes.com/**

The Bible is a strong supporter of observational learning. People watch Christians and learn more from what they do rather than what they say.

The writer to Proverbs, presumably King Solomon, said, *I applied my heart to what I observed and learned a lesson from what I saw* (Proverbs 24:32).

The writer in http://www.letgodbetrue.com/ wrote;

You can learn wisdom by others' mistakes. Observation and analysis are great teachers, and Solomon was a master at both (Ecclesiastes 1:12-14; 2:11-13). It is your duty to learn from the mistakes of others and to teach your children to do so as well.

Of course, you can also learn wisdom by observing the good choices and actions of wise men (Psalm 37:37; Philippians 3:17). It is a helpful habit to watch and identify the character or conduct that makes a man either foolish or wise. It reinforces the rules of wisdom.

Are there profitable lessons by observing good men? Solomon saw that those who fear God are successful and should be followed in life. The Hall of Faith in Hebrews 11 provides a great cloud of witnesses proving the profit of believing and obeying God (Hebrews 11:2; 12:1). And the Lord Jesus Christ, who suffered willingly to obey God, is now sitting at God's right hand with great honor and glory (Hebrews 12:2; Psalm

16:8-11). It is your duty and privilege today to follow his perfect example and obtain God's blessings.

> —http://www.letgodbetrue.com/proverbs/
> commentaries/24_32.php

The Bible clearly states that we are to learn from others by observing their behaviours. the great cloud of witnesses is an example of Christians learning by observing.

> *Therefore, since we are surrounded by such a great cloud of witnesses, let us throw off everything that hinders and the sin that so easily entangles. And let us run with perseverance the race marked out for us, fixing our eyes on Jesus, the pioneer and perfecter of faith.*
>
> —Hebrews 12:1-3

We are to observe these great witnesses and learn from them in how they lived and how they died.

A few sayings on observation from: https://www.brainyquote.com/

- "I believe that you can always learn from observation" (Tamara Tunie).
- "If you make listening and observation your occupation you will gain much more than you can by talk" (Robert Baden-Powell).
- "People's minds are changed through observation and not through argument" (Will Rogers).
- "All ideas come about through some sort of observation; it sparks an attitude or emotion" (Graham Chapman).
- "Accuracy of observation is the equivalent of accuracy of thinking" (Wallace Stevens)
- "To become an academic expert takes years of studying. Academic experts are experts in how and what others have done. They use case studies and observation to understand a subject" (Simon Sinek).

(https://www.brainyquote.com/quotes/keywords/observation.html)

Observation is a key to learning in the African context. It is the beginning of traditional learning. As teachers, we need to remember that students are observing us in what we say and what we do.

Imitation

The Rev. Bitrus Thaba says, "What is imitation? Imitation is from the Greek word meaning 'to imitate' or 'to emulate' (mimeomai)" (Janvier and Thaba 1993. p.59).

Bryan R. Warnick, Assistant Professor of Philosophy of Education at the Ohio State University USA writes,

> Imitation and Education provides an in-depth reassessment of learning by example that places imitation in a larger social context . . . of ancient educational thought and startling breakthroughs in the fields of cognitive science, psychology, and philosophy to reconsider how we learn from the lives of others.
>
> —http://www.sunypress.edu/p-4594-imitation-and-education.aspx

> A growing body of scientific literature has described indigenous ways of learning, in different cultures and countries. Learning in indigenous communities is a process that involves all members in the community.
>
> The learning styles that children use in their indigenous schooling are the same ones that occur in their community context. These indigenous learning styles often include: observation, imitation, use of narrative story telling.
>
> —https://en.wikipedia.org/wiki/Indigenous_education

The Bible and imitation

Both the Bible and African culture, place a great importance on imitation as a learning tool. The Rev. Bitrus Thaba outlines the biblical pattern of imitation. He writes;

> First, God, as object of imitation, Ephesians 5:1
> *Follow God's example, therefore, as dearly loved children*
> is the only specific command to imitation in the New Testament.
>
> Second, Christ is to be the object of imitation. Twice, in Paul's letters, is the imitation of Christ expressed in terms under consideration. In 1 Corinthians 11:1
> *Follow my example, as I follow the example of Christ.*
> Paul claims to be an imitator of Christ and in 1 Thessalonians 1:6
> *You became imitators of us and of the Lord, for you welcomed the message in the midst of severe suffering with the joy given by the Holy Spirit.*
>
> Third, Paul is given as the object of imitation. Most of the uses of the terms imitation in Paul involves himself as the example to be imitated. In 1 Thessalonians 1:6 imitating Paul and Christ are linked together.
>
> Fourth, others are given as the object of imitation. In 1Thessalonians 2:14
> *For you, brothers and sisters, became imitators of God's churches in Judea, which are in Christ Jesus.*
> —Janvier and Thaba. *Discipleship; A West African Perspective.*
> Kaduna, Nigeria. Baraka Press. 1993. p. 59

Bible study on imitation

At this point, let us review several Bible verses on the importance of imitation.

- *Therefore I urge you to imitate me* (1 Corinthians 4:16).

  > Paul is urging people to mimic his life because he practices the things that he presses upon the Corinthians. If they watch him, they will see that he does not glory in Greek wisdom. He does not live for human praise. Rather, he calls the Corinthians to a radically Christ like life.
  > —https://bible.org/seriespage/12-tough-and-tender-1-corinthians-46-21

- *We did this, not because we do not have the right to such help, but in order to offer ourselves as a model for you to imitate* (2 Thessalonians 3:9).

  > The apostle was always deeply concerned about his own example of Christ-likeness for he knew that a student will become like his teacher (Luke 6:40).
  > —http://bible.org/serispage/9-final-exhortations-regarding-idleness-church-2-thes-36-18

- *We do not want you to become lazy, but to imitate those who through faith and patience inherit what has been promised* (Hebrews 6:12). He hoped that every one of them would learn from the example of the faithful (http://www.soundofgrace.com/hebrews/h6v09-12.htm).

- *Remember your leaders, who spoke the word of God to you. Consider the outcome of their way of life and imitate their faith* (Hebrews 13:7).

  > There are three marks of a spiritual leader:
  > 1. Man of Truth (He believes the entire/whole truth of Scripture).
  > 2. Man of Trust.
  > 3. Man with a Clean Testimony.
  > —https://www.sermoncentral.com/sermons/how-to-recognize-a-spiritual-leader-mike-fogerson-sermon-on-spiritual-leadership-190530?page=2

> *Dear friend, do not imitate what is evil but what is good. Anyone who does what is good is from God. Anyone who does what is evil has not seen God.*

—3 John 1:11

The teaching of 3 John 11 is, as Christians, we are under obligation to be careful what model we imitate! As a Christian, I have accepted the duty to act under the influence of good role models, not evil.

—http://www.bible.ca/ef/expository-3-john-11.htm

Some sayings on imitation

- The theologians have recognized that the ideal is the imitation of God. If we be a part of such an organic thing, this thing is God to us, as I am God to the cells that compose me.

  —Charles Fort

- "Admiration of great men, living or dead, naturally evokes imitation of them in a greater or less degree" (Samuel Smiles. https://www.brainyquote.com/quotes/keywords/imitation.html)

- When the imitation of Christ does not mean to live a life like Christ, but to live your life as authentically as Christ lived his, then there are many ways and forms in which a man can be a Christian.

  —Henri J.M. Nouwen

- "Imitation is not just the sincerest form of flattery - it's the sincerest form of learning" (George Bernard Shaw).

- "Imitation is human intelligence in its most dynamic aspect" (René Girard).

- "Imitate the traits of your creator" (Sunday Adelaja).

- "My works are an imitation of my own past and present" (Barbara Hepworth).

- Of course as children, we all, in all cultures and societies, learn behavior from observation, imitation, and encouragement of various kinds. So by the suggestion made, we all 'pretend' most of the time.

  —Gary Gygax

- "If one imitates the upright, one becomes upright. If one imitates the crooked, one becomes crooked" (Christie Watson, http://www.goodreads.com/quotes/tag/imitation?page=3)

Participation

Participation is the act of engaging in an activity. It is being a doer and not a spectator and is the third part of our African learning styles study.

Commentating on African children's learning style, Onike Rahaman comments;

Children also engaged in participatory education through ceremonies, rituals, recitation and demonstration. Proverbs and riddles constituted a formidable intellectual exercise. The proverbs are important to Yoruba because it brings out meaning out of obscure points in conversation and argument.

In general, the system of indigenous education had a close link with social life. It gave a progressive development, which conformed with the successive stages of physical, emotional and mental development of child.

In conclusion, I will like to dismiss the contention that there was no education before the introduction of missionary education in Nigeria. There was informal system of education which were being employed to transmit cultural value and help the children's developmental, intellectual, emotional skills and experiences.

—https://www.google.com/#safe=active&q=definition+of +education+by+fafunwa+1974

Christianity is a participatory spiritual reality. Baptism, communion, prayer, evangelism, preaching and compassion ministry all point to Christianity working best when its members participate in the work the Lord is doing. For example;

- Again Jesus said, *Peace be with you! As the Father has sent me, I am sending you* (John 20:21). Jesus did not teach apart from actions that his followers were to do. In John 20:21 Jesus used himself as an example of ministry and said he was sending out his followers on the same journey; action!

- > *But you will receive power when the Holy Spirit comes on you; and you will be my witnesses in Jerusalem, and in all Judea and Samaria, and to the ends of the earth.*
  >
  > —Acts 1:8

Power was given for a purpose, to evangelize the world as witnesses for Christ. We often focus on the filling of the Holy Spirit in this verse but the task is to win the world for Christ.

- > *Therefore go and make disciples of all nations, baptizing them in the name of the Father and of the Son and of the Holy Spirit, and teaching them to obey everything I have commanded you. And surely I am with you always, to the very end of the age.*
  >
  > —Matthew 28:19-20

The educational task in this verse is twofold. First to make disciples and second to teach them the commands of Jesus. Where is this to be done? It is to be done in all the world both locally and internationally.

> Tell me; I'll forget. Show me; I may remember. But involve me and I'll understand.
>
> **—Chinese proverb. http://www.sermonillustrations.com/a-z/l/learning.htm**

How to teach using observation, imitation and participation

- Provide teaching styles that role model observation, imitation, and participation. Dr. Ogunbiyi Oluranti Ph.D. of Lagos State University, states,

  > Research findings reveal that while learning styles are varied, teaching styles are rigid and one-directional. Attempts must be made to match teaching with learning styles.
  >
  > —http://www.bjournal.co.uk/BJASS.aspx

- Provide activities in the classroom such as dramas to give students the opportunity to observe and then act out a problem through imitation and participation.

- Field trips can be used for students to observe activities such as preaching, teaching, sports, and many other types of activities.

- Case studies where students study a problem, make observations and draw conclusions from their own participation in mimicking the case study.

- Practicum work gives students the opportunity to observe each other and then imitate through participation.

- Western education emphasizes "knowing." ATE has traditional emphasized "doing." In your teaching, try to have a mix between knowing and doing by making more practical exercises for students as well as normal lectures.

Conclusion

It is important to remember that students come from a cultural context and we should use their traditional learning styles where possible. Rather than a strictly western style of education as a lecture, ATE aspects can easily be added to the teachers' methods of communication. This will work with most classes in Bible Colleges and seminaries. For example, in a course on teaching methods, I sent students out to observe teachers on different levels from secondary schools, church and higher education settings to make observations which I hoped would lead to imitation and ultimately participation by the students on what they learned.

Our goal as teachers should be to be the most effective teachers we can be. This comes through a mix of Western and African styles of learning that better fit the cultural context of our classrooms.

Remember that students are a mix of learning styles. While they were born into a language and cultural context they are studying in another language and cultural context. A visionary teacher teaches from a broad set of methods designed to help students from different learning styles to get the most out of their teaching.

Study Questions

1. Should a teacher incorporate African traditional teaching methods into his or her teaching style? Why or why not?
2. Give an example of how you have experienced the ATE pattern of observation, imitation and participation in your own education.
3. Give some examples of how a teacher can use observation, imitation and participation in the classroom.

CHAPTER 10

PRINCIPLES OF LEARNING FROM THE BIBLE

Although it is good to examine Western and African styles of learning, it is also good to explore what God says about how we learn. We must remember, though, that the culture of the Bible is different than our culture today. Nevertheless, we can discover timeless principles from the Bible that still apply today. It is best to combine the biblical teachings on learning with modern educational thinking on learning. We can learn many things from both sources.

I see five main categories, or principles, for understanding what the Bible has to say about how we learn. They are:

1.	The centrality of the word of God

2.	The need for a relationship with God, Jesus and the Holy Spirit.

3.	Learning from each other.

4.	Training yourself.

5.	Learning through the family.

These five principles will be studied one at a time. Before studying the positive aspects of what the Bible has to say about learning, two negatives will be studied. Paul tells Timothy that it is possible to be, *always learning but never able to come to a knowledge of the truth* (2 Timothy 3:7).

> Observation, more than books and experience, are the prime educators.
> —**Albert Einstein in: https:// www.brainyquote.com/**

Paul told Timothy that learning is not necessarily the goal of education, but discovering truth is. It is possible to be a learner but not a discoverer of truth. As teachers we need to help students discover truth.

Second, the writer of the Book of Ecclesiastes says, *Be warned, my son, of anything in addition to them. Of making many books there is no end, and much study wearies the body* (Ecclesiastes 12:12).

> I prefer physical exhaustion over mental fatigue any day.
> —**Clotilde Hesme in: https:// www.brainyquote.com/**

How many books does a good library hold and how many of those books can one read in a lifetime? As a person grows older and the eyes start to fade, reading becomes even more of a chore. We should begin our Christian lives with reading and seeking the truth, but then live out what we read especially in God's word. The following five topics are God's pattern for learning.

The centrality of the word of God

The first principle in studying about God's pattern for learning is the centrality of the word of God. The word of God is God's truth written down for our learning. The word of God is a great teacher and no matter how many times you read it you can gain valuable insights. Bible reading is a great learning tool. Numerous Bible verses testify to the teaching-learning power of the Bible. For example:

1.   *All Scripture is God-breathed and is useful for teaching, rebuking, correcting and training in righteousness, so that the servant of God may be thoroughly equipped for every good work.*

    —2 Timothy 3:16-17

Paul tells Timothy to focus on the word of God, as it is a valuable tool for teaching and learning. The word of God is a great tool for helping newer and older believers in their walk with the Lord. A visionary teacher needs to equip students for the world of work and ministry and the word of God does that.

2.   *For the word of God is alive and active. Sharper than any double-edged sword, it penetrates even to dividing soul and spirit, joints and marrow; it judges the thoughts and attitudes of the heart.*

    —Hebrews 4:12

The writer of the Book of Hebrews says that the word of God has a special teaching-learning aspect to it. It is the Holy Spirit, like a surgeon, cutting through the wrong ideas about what the heart says is true. It is a correcting ministry of the Holy Spirit in the lives of people.

> I am blessed to receive a word from God every day in receiving the scriptures and reading the scriptures. And God speaks through the Bible.
>
> **—Ted Cruz in: https:// www.brainyquote.com/**

3.   *For everything that was written in the past was written to teach us, so that through the endurance taught in the Scriptures and the encouragement they provide we might have hope.*

—Romans 15:4

Paul tells the Romans that the written word is a good teaching-learning tool which will encourage us and gives us hope. It is good to use a variety of books to teach students but the word of God is the best book to draw illustrations and teachings from.

4.   *Keep this Book of the Law always on your lips; meditate on it day and night, so that you may be careful to do everything written in it. Then you will be prosperous and successful.*

—Joshua 1:8

Students today are concerned about success and prosperity in themselves and for their families. Joshua gives a formula for that success. He says that the word of God is a powerful tool for student success. Focusing on the word of God leads to focusing on God himself and that is the pattern for success in the Christian life.

The need for a relationship with God, Jesus and the Holy Spirit.

The second principle in the biblical plan for Christian growth is the need for a relationship with God, Jesus and the Holy Spirit. For example;

Relationship with God

- *The fear of the Lord is the beginning of knowledge, but fools despise wisdom and instruction* (Proverbs 1:7). The biblical plan for learning begins with God. When we ultimately honour God with our lives, he becomes our teacher. According to this verse, wise men and women seek the Lord, wisdom and instruction for a victorious life.

> The highest knowledge is the knowledge of God.
>
> **—McKenzie p.210**

- *I will instruct you and teach you in the way you should go; I will counsel you with my loving eye on you* (Psalm 32:8). When God instructs you, the path becomes clear. He counsels us by way of his loving eye. The greatest instructor is God.
- *If any of you lack wisdom, you should ask God, who gives generously to all without finding fault, and it will be given to you.*

  —James 1:5

Wisdom is a gift of God. Every student wants a good measure of wisdom. The pattern is first to ask God for wisdom and second to wait for God to give it freely. This is God's way of learning, to ask for wisdom.

> You can buy education but wisdom comes from God.
>
> **—McKenzie p.208**

Relationship with Jesus

Besides a relationship with God the Father, the biblical learning plan is a relationship with Jesus Christ. Several verses illustrate this:

- *Take my yoke upon you and learn from me, for I am gentle and humble in heart, and you will find rest for your souls.*

  —Matthew 11:29

Jesus makes the student an offer, to learn directly from him. The benefit of Jesus as the teacher is peace and rest for our inner person, our soul. The writer of *Newlife Commentary* writes:

> Jesus wants us to come to him and learn from him in a continuing relationship. He will equip us, teach us, and guide us to be effective in life and service, if we allow him. If we come to Jesus and do things his way, in partnership and communion with him, he promises that we will find rest and refreshment for our souls. In the process, we will become more like our rabbi Jesus: gentle and humble in heart.
>
> —http://newlife.id.au/christian-living/come-to-me/

Jesus said,

> *If you keep my commands, you will remain in my love, just as I have kept my Father's commands and remain in his love. I have told you this so that my joy may be in you and that your joy may be complete. My command is this: Love each other as I have loved*

*you. Greater love has no one that this: to lay down one's life for
one's friends. You are my friends if you do what I command.*

—John 15:10-14

The teachings of Jesus are clear. A disciple is a learner and needs to
do several things. First, remain in the love of Christ. Second, love
each other. Third, be willing to lay down your life for your friends.
Fourth, obey the commands of Jesus. What is the reward for this?
Jesus says your joy will be made complete.

- *Therefore everyone who hears these words of mine and puts them
  into practice is like a wise man who built his house on the rock.*

—Matthew 7:24

Real biblical learning is when you put into practice the things Jesus
taught and is still teaching us today.

Relationship with the Holy Spirit

We learn through our relationship with the Holy Spirit. Several Bible
verses illustrate this:

*But the Advocate, the Holy Spirit, whom the Father will send in my
name, will teach you all things and will remind you of everything
I have said to you.*

—John 14:26

Students need to be taught, and also reminded of what is important.
Jesus said the ministry of the Holy Spirit was to teach and remind
them of priorities in the Christian walk. Jesus' words were spoken
with authority. Note that the Father sent the Holy Spirit in Jesus'
name to teach all things and remember all things. This is the strongest
statement in the Bible on learning.

Church minister, Martin G. Collins writes,

No man, by scholarship, human reason, or intelligence can comprehend the whole truth of God apart from the Holy Spirit. Only by the intervention of the Spirit are we called to understand it. God, by divine revelation through the help of the Spirit, opens our minds to the "mysteries" of truth, allowing us to discern what is truly vital to our salvation.

—http://www.bibletools.org/index.cfm/fuseaction/
bible.show/sVerseID/26695/eVerseID/26695

What do we learn from these verses? Our relationship with the godhead, the Trinity, is strategic to our learning, especially learning spiritual matters. Each member of the Trinity has his own teaching patterns. As disciples, we have a responsibility to understand and be obedient to each member of the godhead in learning what he has to teach us.

Learn from each other

The third principle in understanding God's programme for our education is to learn from each other. We have more to learn from each other than we realize. The Apostle Paul writes; *I myself am convinced, my brothers and sisters, that you yourselves are full of goodness, filled with knowledge and competent to instruct one another* (Romans 15:14). Paul says we are competent to teach one another. This takes place every time we sit with someone for discipleship, have devotions with our families, or do ministry in church. We are teaching each other.

Again, Paul teaches us on how we can learn from each other saying,

Let the message of Christ dwell among you richly as you teach and admonish one another with all wisdom through psalms, hymns, and songs from the Spirit, singing to God with gratitude in your hearts.

—Colossians 3:16

When we admonish someone, we warn them or reprimand them, or urge them onto great heights of Christian living.

Paul says we can build each other up by sharing our faith with each other.

> *I long to see you so that I may impart to you some spiritual gift to make you strong— that is, that you and I may be mutually encouraged by each other's faith.*
>
> —Romans 1:11-12

Often I am encouraged and build up when a brother or sister shares a story of how God has been faithful to them.

> You need an attitude of service. You're not just serving yourself. You help others to grow up and you grow with them.
> **—David Green in: https:// www.brainyquote.com/**

Here are a few other verses that encourage us to teach each other:

- *And let us consider how we may spur one another on toward love and good deeds* (Hebrews 10:24).
- *Therefore encourage one another and build each other up, just as in fact you are doing* (1 Thessalonians 5:11).
- *Now about your love for one another we do not need to write to you, for you yourselves have been taught by God to love each other* (1 Thessalonians 4:9).

Train yourself

The fourth principle of learning to understand God's programme of education is to train yourself. I have loved the teachers in my life who have made an impact on me to strive for greater learning. However, at some point we have to learn to teach ourselves. Babies need to be fed by someone else but only for so long. Then they learn use their fingers or a fork and spoon and feed themselves. The Bible encourages us to be self-feeders, that is, to teach and train ourselves. For example;

- *Have nothing to do with godless myths and old wives' tales; rather, train yourself to be godly* (1 Timothy 4:7). Paul tells Timothy that a sign of maturity in the Christian life is to be able to train, or feed, yourself. Someone is not always present to instruct us so it is best to be a self-feeder.

Commentator Kevin Pierpont writes,

> Paul goes on in the end of verse seven to encourage Timothy to train himself to be godly. Godliness is not automatic, is it? If you've become a child of God by receiving Christ as your Lord and Saviour, you didn't instantaneously achieve Godliness. If you want to lead a Godly life it takes discipline and diligence on your part you need to actively pursue Godliness.
>
> —http://kevinpierpont.com/be-an-example-to-the-believers/

A second verse that encourages us to teach ourselves is Jude 1:20-21 where Jude states, But you, dear friends, by building yourselves up in your most holy faith and praying in the Holy Spirit keeping yourselves in God's love as you wait for the mercy of our Lord Jesus Christ to bring you to eternal life. Several other verses teach the same idea of training-teaching yourself;

- *You, then, who teach others, do you not teach yourself?* (Romans 2:21).
- Now the Berean Jews were of more noble character than those in Thessalonica, for they received the message with great eagerness

and examined the Scriptures every day to see if what Paul said was true (Acts 17:11).

Paul was the great Apostle and the Berean Christians accepted him but wanted to study for themselves to see if what Paul said was true.

• *Let the wise listen and add to their learning, and let the discerning get guidance* (Proverbs 1:5). Wise people teach themselves and add to their learning.

Family education

The family is the final training ground for this study on biblical principles for learning. The family is probably the greatest learning "school" in existence today. More things are learned in the family and more of life's patterns are set in motion from the family than most people realize or give credit for.

> I am blessed to have so many great things in my life-family, friends and God. All will be in my thoughts daily.
> —**By Lil' Kim in: https:// www.brainyquote.com/**

The biblical pattern for learning includes the family. For example;

The role of the parents

The role of the parents is obvious. In many ways, I am my dad. That includes hobbies, interests, priorities, foods, humour, handling money, cloths, cars, sports and many other things. It is true, "Like father like son." The mother's role is equally important and influential. I have my mother's attitudes, likes and dislikes. In many ways, I am my parents. This warns us to be extra special in raising our kids. Both quantity time and quality time are needed in child rearing. What does the Bible say about the role of the parents?

- *Listen, my son, to your father's instruction and do not forsake your mother's teaching. They are a garland to grace your head and a chain to adorn your neck.*

                                                            —Proverbs 1:8-9

Both the father and the mother play a major role in the spiritual training and cultural training of the children. Proverbs 6:20 echo's this thought; *My son, keep your father's command and do not forsake your mother's teaching* (Proverbs 6:20).

- *A fool spurns a parent's discipline, but whoever heeds correction shows prudence* (Proverbs 15:5). Parental teaching and corrections are vital is the successful raising of children.

> At the end of the day, the most overwhelming key to a child's success is the positive involvement of parents.
> **—Jane D. Hull in https:// www.brainyquote.com**

The role of the father is given out in the New Testament stating; *Fathers, do not exasperate your children; instead, bring them up in the training and instruction of the Lord* (Ephesians 6:4). Proverbs adds, *Listen, my sons, to a father's instruction; pay attention and gain understanding* (Proverbs 4:1).

The role of the mother is also important. Timothy was led to the Lord because of his mother.

I am reminded of your sincere faith, which first lived in your grandmother Lois and in your mother Eunice and, I am persuaded, now lives in you also

—2 Timothy 1:5

Three generations of people became Christians because of the influence of their mothers. The teaching role of the mother, in the home is spelled out in Proverbs.

She speaks with wisdom and faithful instruction is on her tongue...
Her children arise and call her blessed; her husband also, and he praises her.

—Proverbs 31:21

A family had four sons. All for sons went into the ministry and were successful preachers. One year at a family gathering someone asked, "Who's the greatest preacher in the family?" The four sons all said, "Our mother!"

Parents are the ultimate role models for children. Every word, movement and action has an effect. No other person or outside force has a greater influence on a child that the parents.

—Bob Keeshan in https:// www.brainyquote.com

The role of Scripture

The classic passage of Scripture on teaching children in the home is from Deuteronomy stating;

- *Here, O Israel: The Lord our God, the Lord is one. Love the Lord your God with all your heart and with all your soul and with*

> *all your strength. These comman∕ments that I give you to∕ay are to be on your hearts. Impress them on your chil∕ren. Talk about them when you sit at home an∕ when you walk along the roa∕, when you lie ∕own an∕ when you get up. Tie them as symbols on your han∕s an∕ bin∕ them on your forehea∕s. Write them on the ∕oorframes of your houses an∕ on your gates,*

—Deuteronomy 6:4-9.

This tells us what God's agenda for helping children to learn Scripture and about the Lord himself is.

- *An∕ how from infancy you have known the Holy Scriptures, which are able to make you wise for salvation through faith in Christ Jesus* (2 Timothy 3:15). Knowing and teaching the Scriptures can lead to the salvation of our children.

Conclusion

Studying the Bible is to attend a free school in life. Everyone should attend two schools. One is the government school. The second school is the school of the Bible. This does not necessarily mean a formal Bible school but more informal and non-formal individual and group Bible study. Our five study goals, in this chapter, have introduced us to the important topics of how God intends us to learn. As a reminder the five principles of biblical learning are;

1.   The centrality of the word of God.
2.   The need for a relationship with God, Jesus and the Holy Spirit.
3.   Learning from each other.
4.   Training yourself.
5.   Learning through the family.

Remember, not everyone learns the same way. Some learn in the home and some learn outside the home. Some learn best by self-study and some learn best in-group studies. Our biblical education-learning style should include Bible knowledge (knowing) as well as action on what we are learning (doing). It includes learning in the family and in the community and church. God's programme for our learning is creative and varied and is blessed by the Holy Spirit.

Study Questions

1. How is the Bible's pattern for learning different from the more formal schooling models of learning?
2. Why are parents the best teachers for real learning?
3. What learning pattern fits you best, self-learning or group learning? Explain your answer.

CHAPTER 11

TEACHER-CENTRED INSTRUCTION OR STUDENT-CENTRED LEARNING?

How much should a teacher spend in lecturing and how much time should each student contribute to his or own learning through dialogue and question and answers with the teacher? This will be discussed in this chapter. We will look at teacher-centred instructing and student-cantered learning.

Teacher-Centred Education

Teaching is a great profession and is a position of great influence. A.P.J. Kalam writes on being a teacher,

> Teaching is a very noble profession that shapes the character, calibre, and future of an individual. If the people remember me as a good teacher, that will be the biggest honour for me.
> —A. P. J. Abdul Kalam in: https://www.brainyquote.com

However, what kind of teachers are we to be? In the teacher-centred instruction the teacher is active and the students are passive. The teacher does all the work. Teachers teach and then says, "Are there any questions?" Some student raises his hand and says, "Sir, will that be on the exam?" In teacher-centred education, students put all of their focus on the teacher. The teacher talks, while the students listen. During activities, students work alone and group work is often discouraged in favour of the individual.

Christian author Michael J. Anthony writes;

> In most traditional schooling situations, the only teaching method used is lecture, or telling. The students are given what the teacher has learned and only experience the information indirectly.
>
> —Michael J. Anthony in: *Christian Education for the 21ˢᵗ Century* p.95

> Learning usually passes through three states. In the beginning you learn the right answers. In the second state you learn the right questions. In the third and final stage you learn which questions are worth asking.
>
> **—http:// www.sermonillustrations.com/a-z/l/ learning.html**

In teacher-centred education the students are viewed as empty vessels that need to be filled up with the knowledge which the teacher has studied for many years. Students absorb the information, write it down in a note book, and give it back to the teacher in the form of exams and term papers. The student is passive and does not say much other than ask a question at the end of the lecture.

Advantages of teacher centred teaching

- When education is teacher-centred, the classroom remains orderly. Students are quiet, and the teacher retains full control of the classroom and its activities.

- Because students learn on their own, they learn to be independent and make their own decisions.

- Because the teacher directs all classroom activities, they don't have to worry that students will miss an important point.

- Assessment of each student is easier as exam grading is clear and simple.

- You can cover more material in less time.

- A teacher-centred style is more familiar to the students and is more culturally acceptable in many contexts.

- It is easier for the teacher to lecture and takes less energy than creative interactive discussions.

(http://education.cu-portland.edu/blog/classroom-resources/which-is-best-teacher-centered-or-student-centered-education/)

Disadvantages of teacher-centred teaching

- When students work alone, they do not learn to work as a community, and communication skills may suffer. Community is not encouraged. Competition is role modelled.

- Teacher-centred instruction can get boring for students. Their minds may wander and they may miss important facts.

- Teacher-centred instruction does not allow students to express themselves, ask questions and direct their own learning.

(With assistance from; http://education.cu-portland.edu/blog/classroom-resources/which-is-best-teacher-centered-or-student-centered-education)

Suggestions if you use the teacher-centred method

- Have students read on the topic before the class if possible. The more they know before they come to class the more familiar with the topic they will be. The lecture will be richer.
- Have a wider purpose than knowledge (information). Ephesians. 3:19 says, *The love of Christ surpasses knowleʻge.*
- Encourage library skills, Internet skills and research skills through assignments.
- Help students to learn to develop skills of research and application.
- Use Power Point where possible. This will help them to "see" as well as "hear."
- Walk around the classroom. Don't be stuck to the lectern.

Student-Centred Learning

Student-Centred learning is called by many different names including; Active learning, student participatory learning, student centred learning, inductive learning, discovery learning or Socratic learning. Both the teacher and student are active in the learning process. Extreme student-centred learning says the students direct all their own learning. This is too extreme for most contexts. I am suggesting a method that is modified where the teacher is still in charge but involves the students in their own learning process.

Student-centred learning puts more of the work on the student rather than the teacher. This puts the student's minds to work and their brains are active. The emphasis is on what the student does rather than on what the teacher does.

The goal of student-centred learning is knowledge plus the development of thinking skills. I have often called it "knowledge plus." Knowledge plus what? Knowledge plus thinking, the development of self-confidence and critical thinking skills. These thinking skills will last a student for a lifetime of work and ministry.

Michael J. Anthony writes,

> The teacher needs to view his or her role as a facilitator who helps bring about learning. This type of leader encourages participation from the student and demonstrates caring and acceptance.
>
> —Michael J. Anthony in *Christian Education for the 21ˢᵗ Century*
> p.95

> The task of the modern educator is not to cut down jungles, but irrigate deserts.
> **—C.S. Lewis in: https://
> www.brainyquote.com**

Anthony adds,

> Transformation occurs when more methods are added to the process. When students not only listen but also practice doing and reflecting, they are much more likely to integrate what they are learning into the own direct experience.
>
> —Michael J. Anthony in: *Christian Education for the 21ˢᵗ
> Century* p.95

When a classroom functions with student-centered learning, students and instructors share the focus. Instead of listening to the teacher exclusively, students and teachers interact together. Group work is encouraged, and students learn to work together and communicate with one another.

In the student-centred classroom, the teacher still plays a key role in designing classroom activities, encouraging student discussions and giving students guidance when necessary. The teacher can still lecture but on a more limited basis. For example, a teacher may introduce a new topic through lecture then ask students to evaluate what was taught. The teacher can use case studies where the teacher reads the case study and then asks students to evaluate the case study and suggest solutions to the problem or problems raised in the case study.

Let's review. Remember that in student-centred learning the teacher is not redundant and still plays an important part in the teaching-learning experience. The big picture of student centred learning is that, "Students gain skills in communication and collaboration, as well as how to take charge of their own learning by asking good questions and being responsible for specific tasks."

—http://education.cu-portland.edu/blog/classroom-resources/which-is-best-teacher-centered-or-student-centered-education/

Advantages of Student-centred learning and teaching

- Students learn important communication and group skills through group work.
- Students learn to direct their own education, ask questions and complete assignments independently.
- Students are more interested in learning activities when they can interact with one another and participate actively in the process.
- Student centred learning is more applicable to their lives and ministries.

- Strengthens student motivation.
- Promotes peer communication.
- Reduces disruptive behaviour.
- Builds student-teacher relationships.
- Promotes discovery/active learning.
- Responsibility for one's own learning.

Disadvantages of student centred learning

- Because students are talking, classrooms are often busy and noisy.
- Teachers must attempt to manage all student's activities at once, which can be difficult when students are working on different stages of the same project.
- Because the teacher does not deliver instruction to all students at once, some students may miss important facts.
- Some students prefer to work alone so group work can become problematic.
- This method does not cover as much material as a lecture.
- This method takes more time to plan questions and more energy to lead the discussions.
- Giving students a grade can be more difficult as discussion is hard to grade.

Suggestions if you want to be more student-centred

- The teacher should use a variety of methods such as lecture, question and answer, group discussions, small group work, debate, seminar presentation and case studies.

- Use a community learning style. Colossians 3:16 says, *Let the message of Christ dwell among you richly as you <u>teach and admonish one another</u> with all wisdom.*

- Give students a chance to present papers and then critique them in class.

- Have materials prepared for students to buy and read before class, and then discuss the papers in class.

- Guide students to learn on their own and develop skills of research and application. 1Timothy 4:7 says, *Have nothing to do with godless myths and old wives' tales; rather, <u>train yourself</u> to be godly.*

- Have a handout and then encourage reflection papers and ask: "What did you learn in this assignment?" Or; "What does this assignment mean to you and your ministry?"

- Send students out for interviews. Rather than read a book written by someone about ministry in the 1980's, send students out to talk to successful men and women in ministry today.

- Give out a short paper and ask students to reflect on what they learned. Have them start with, "I learned . . ."

Teachers of the 21st Century

I conducted a survey among graduate students at a large evangelical seminary in Nigeria. I asked in the student survey, "How can seminary teachers be more dynamic in the classroom? That is, how can they make their teaching more exciting?" The student responded as follows:

- Most of our seminary teachers use the lecture method. But students learn differently so they should employ the use of other teaching methods like discussion and question and answer methods.

- Teaching can be made so exciting by applying the various teaching methods so that no one will be left behind.

- Give room to students who have made in-depth study of a particular topic to give the class at least a 10 minute lecture while the teacher supervises.
- They can be more dynamic by giving enough time for discussion in class.
- They can constantly draw the student's attention as to what is the relevance and importance the course being taught is (purpose driven teaching).
- The teaching methods need to fit the instructor and the situation.
- Allow for dramas, group discussion and paper presentations in class.
- The teachers should use a projector on occasion.
- They need to relate the principles to modern life.
- They need to vary the teaching styles periodically.
- Teachers should make sure that their classes are participatory and encourage student participation. *Keep putting into practice all you have learne* (Philippians 4:9).
- Teachers should create a context for learning in which students can become engaged in interactive activities that encourage and facilitate learning.
- Give clear instructions to the students in class and for assignments.
- Lecturers should produce lecture notes (for each student) and focus on the use of the Bible in class.
- I sat in a course two times and the teacher used the same notes both times.
- Seminary teachers should work hard to research every time.
- Be friendly and accessible to the students.

Students of the 21st Century

As part of the survey, I asked seminary students to reflect on how they were different from the students of 20 years ago. Here are their responses:

- "Twenty years ago students were spoon fed. But current students make findings themselves which increase their learning."
- "The use of computers, the Internet and cell phones are an added advantage to students of 20 years ago."
- "The learning environment is improved and the availability of information and materials, and IT aids are helpful. Both teachers and students have a lot of materials at their disposal."
- "Students of today are more open and outgoing than 20 years ago."
- "Students before were more godly."
- "The students of 20 years ago came from a good educational background."
- "The challenges of current students are more than those of 20 years ago.""

Points gained from the survey

- Students of the 21st century participate more in their own education and balance knowledge with skills. They are better thinkers, use information technology and are better problem solvers.
- The students of today are more aggressive learners, especially on the higher levels.
- Students of today and tomorrow are hopefully dong more thinking, read at home, come to class and want to discuss issues rather than always hear a lecture.
- Teachers of today and tomorrow are hopefully encouraging thinking and applying their teachings to the issues of the day

through discussion, question and answer methods, case studies, student presentations and debates.

- Teachers of tomorrow need to be more global in their experience, use the Internet, are comfortable with discussion, help to facilitate holistic learning and are aware of what is going on in the world.

> A good teacher can inspire hope, ignite the imagination, and instill a love of learning.
> **—Brad Henry in: https:// www.brainyquote.com**

Conclusion

This chapter asks the question, "Which is a better system to use in the classroom; the teacher-centred method or the student-centred method?" It depends on several factors such as:

- The personality of the teacher. Teaching methods are sometimes conditioned by the teacher's personality. Not all teachers are comfortable with the more open style of question and answer or dialogue method of teaching. Find your style as a teacher and experiment with other styles.
- The type of students in the class. Not everyone learns the same way. Some students like to interact with other students whereas some students like to read and learn alone or from the teacher only. Have a variety of learning activities in each class.
- The subject being taught affects the teaching style. Teaching methods are sometimes conditioned by the subject being taught (Greek or Homiletics call for different styles of teaching than preaching or evangelism classes).

- The cultural context of the school. Every school sits in a cultural context. Some contexts rely on more rote learning or lecture method. If your school sits in that type of context shifting to a more student-centred type of learning may be too much of a shock for students to accept.

Recommendations

- Use a mix of styles. Lecture for part of the class but have students participate through discussion, debates, question and answer.
- Since teaching styles are the methods and approaches teachers feel most comfortable with, it might be difficult to change completely to a different approach from what they are used to. But to be effective teachers of the 21st century we need to be prepared for the different types of students we have in each class and have different methods to maximize their learning. I suggest teachers have a variety of methods so that no student is left behind.
- Mix written exams with practical exercises such as classroom presentations. This will better test for the variety of students in every classroom.
- Apply your teaching to the issues of the day in the home, school, church and society. Students are excited to learn how to deal with life's problems and this will better prepare them for life after school.

Warnings

1. To be totally student-centred, that is, completely self directed, would be a mistake. No matter how high a youth climbs a tree he cannot see as far as the elders.
2. To be student-centred is not totally cultural. It may not fit the image of a teacher in every context. We may lose the respect of the students especially on the diploma and BA levels.

3.   It can be threatening to the teacher when they ask a question and do not get a response.
4.   The level of the class (diploma, BA, MA), the course and the number of students in the class often determine the amount of student-centred teaching you can do.
5.   It takes time to plan and energy to do debates and question and answer. It is easier and takes less energy to read a paper.
6.   Not every teacher has an enthusiastic personality.
7.   The class you are teaching may determine the style of teaching.

Study Questions

1.   Will using student-centred teaching methods work in your cultural context? Explain your answer.
2.   What are some of the dangers of using the student-centred method of teaching?
3.   What are some of the advantages of a teacher-centred method of teaching?

CHAPTER 12

INDUCTIVE AND SOCRATIC

A few years ago, I attended a seminar on education. After the teacher introduced his name and background he said, "I am inductive and Socratic." Some of the conference participants were confused as to what the teacher meant by being "inductive and Socratic." He was referring to his style of teaching. Those two words and their meanings will be explored in this chapter.

Inductive

Inductive teaching has been around for centuries. However, it was not practiced much until the late 20th century.

Case study #11

In a class on Pastoral Theology, a teacher entered the large classroom and was set to teach. The students were ready to write down every word the teacher said as they knew the teacher would test them with an exam later in the term. The teacher greeted the students and then began to teach. He introduced the topic for the day in the form of a case study. The case study was about a problem that his church was having. The teacher gave a short hand-out paper, and taught for about 15 minutes. The teacher then presented several ways of dealing with the problem. Then the students were shocked when the teacher asked them what they thought about the problem and what they suggested the church do about the problem. A lively discussion followed on the church problem. Some of the students had been pastors already and had experienced the same problem in their church. Students were challenged to clarify their own position on the problem. The class ended on a lively note and the students went out excited and continued to discuss the problem even after the class was over.

What is inductive teaching?

The above case study is an example of inductive teaching. Inductive teaching follows the student-centred idea of teaching. A teacher using an inductive teaching method introduces the topic and presents examples to illuminate the topic. Students then form conclusions based on the discussions of the examples.

> Having been an educator for so many years I know that all a good teacher can do is set a context, raise questions or enter into a kind of dialogue relationship with their students.
> —**Godfrey Reggio in: https:// www.brainyquote.com**

The inductive method is not limited to the classroom and is good for discovery-style Bible study. Dr. Julie Gorman writes that inductive Bible study is,

> A methodological approach to the study of scripture. After previewing the whole passage, the student observes with careful focus the exact words and phrases of a

biblical text and proceeds to logical, generalized conclusions based on examination of those observed particulars. The inductive process consists of three major steps: observation, interpretation, and application.

—Gorman in: *Anthony* p. 358

Case study #12

Throughout the years, I have used inductive teaching methods to teach students concepts and generalizations. I present students with data, ask them to make observations of that data, and on the basis of those observations, I ask students to state the concept or generalization that I'm teaching. I have found this to be an effective teaching strategy because it encourages participation, which helps any activity to be more interesting. As you know, the more interesting an activity is, the easier it is to get students focused and involved in the lesson. The inductive teaching method is also effective for developing perceptual and observational skills. Students not only learn content but they learn how to process data and how to use it to arrive at appropriate conclusions. This teaching method involves three general initiatives: planning the activity, executing the activity, and evaluating the outcome.

—https://www.dailyteachingtools.com/teaching-methods.html

Did Jesus ever use the inductive method? Yes, in Matthew 16:13-16, which states,

When Jesus came to the region of Caesarea Philippi, he asked his disciples, "Who do people say the Son of Man is?" They replied, "Some say John the Baptist; others say Elijah; and still others, Jeremiah or one of the prophets." "But what about you?" he asked. "Who do you say I am?" Simon Peter answered, "You are the Messiah, the Son of the living God."

Jesus did not start with the conclusion and then lecture with proofs of who He was. Instead he led Peter to think it through and make the conclusion himself on who Jesus was.

Dr. Duane Elmer commenting on Jesus' use of the inductive method writes,

> Jesus would send the disciples out and not see them until they returned, at which time He asked them to talk about their experience. The simple point here is that Jesus frequently taught inductively. In the context of designed inductive experience, His telling became much more powerful.
> —Elmer, in *Gangel: The Christian Educator's Handbook on Adult Education.* Grand Rapids, MI. Baker Books. 1993. p.135

What is deductive teaching?

To better understand inductive teaching we will look briefly at deductive teaching. The opposite of inductive teaching is deductive teaching. Deductive teaching is a valuable teaching style that has been used for centuries. It is teacher-centred and works well in certain educational contexts. A deductive teacher presents a truth and then supports that truth using different examples. A student writing a deductive term paper presents his or her conclusion after a brief introduction and then spends the following pages supporting that conclusion. In deductive teaching, "the teacher gives the students a new concept, explains it, and then has the students practice using the concept" (https://sites.educ.ualberta.ca/staff/olenka.bilash/Best%20of%20Bilash/inductivedeductive.html).

The lecture method is a form of deductive teaching. Dr. Ken Gangel suggests the following for better deductive-lecturing:[1]

---

[1]Ken Gangel in: *24 Ways to Improve Your Teaching.* Eugene, Oregon. Victor Books. 1974. p.14.

1. Combine the lecture with audience involvement methods such as discussion, question and answer, debates.
2. Support the lecture with visuals.
3. Have a clear and simple outline for the lecture.
4. Practice good principles of speaking.
5. Emphasize important points.
6. Use interesting illustrations.
7. Specify clear objectives.
8. Produce a photocopy of notes.

Did Jesus ever use the deductive method? Yes he did in the Sermon on the Mount.

> *Now when Jesus saw the crowds, he went up on a mountainside and sat down. His disciples came to him, and he began to teach them. He said:*
>
> > *Blessed are the poor in spirit,*
> > *for theirs is the kingdom of heaven.*
> > *Blessed are those who mourn,*
> > *for they will be comforted.*
> > *Blessed are the meek,*
> > *for they will inherit the earth.*
>
> —Matthew 5:1-5

Jesus was the master teacher and knew which method was best for each different context he was teaching in.

Inductive-deductive debate

Which method of teaching should be used, the inductive or deductive? Dennis Sheridan writes,

> Inductive learning is frequently contrasted with deductive learning, the process of moving from general truth to specific

facts. Most Christian educators would agree that induction and deduction can be complementary and that learning is a complex phenomenon that may be understood as utilizing both inductive and deductive processes.

—Anthony, p.359

> Our best teachers do more than impart facts and figures. They inspire and encourage students and instill a true desire to learn. That's a fine art in itself.
> **—Sonny Perdue in: https:// www.brainyquote.com**

Education writer Olenka Bilash writes,

Two very distinct and opposing instructional approaches are inductive and deductive. Both approaches can offer certain advantages, but the biggest difference is the role of the teacher. In a deductive classroom, the teacher conducts lessons by introducing and explaining concepts to students, and then expecting students to complete tasks to practice the concepts; this approach is very teacher-centred. Conversely, inductive instruction is a much more student-centred approach.

—https://sites.educ.ualberta.ca/staff/olenka.bilash/Best%20of %20Bilash/inductivedeductive.html

Socratic

What does it mean to be a "Socratic teacher?" Being a Socratic teacher means following the teaching methods of the great Greek philosopher and teacher Socrates.

Socrates

Socrates was a renowned Greek philosopher who was born around 470 BC during the time of Ezra and Nehemiah. He was an educational philosopher who laid the groundwork for the Western systems of logic and philosophy. Socrates married and had fathered three sons. He died in 399 BC.

Socratic teaching method

Socrates had his own revolutionary teaching method. It was:

> A pedagogical technique in which a teacher does not give information directly but instead asks a series of questions, with the result that the student comes either to the desired knowledge by answering the questions or to a deeper awareness of the limits of knowledge.
>
> —http://www.thefreedictionary.com/

> Employ your time in improving yourself by other men's writings, so that you shall gain easily what others have laboured hard for.
> **—Socrates in: https://www.brainyquote.com**

For Socrates, the city of Athens was a classroom and he went about asking questions of the elite and common man alike, seeking to arrive at political and ethical truths. Socrates didn't lecture about what he knew. In fact, he claimed to be ignorant because he had no ideas, but wise because he recognized his own ignorance. He asked questions of his fellow Athenians in a dialectic method, the Socratic Method, which compelled the audience to think through a problem to a logical conclusion. Sometimes the answer seemed so obvious it made Socrates' opponents look foolish. For this, he was admired by some and vilified by others (https://www.biography.com).

> To know, is to know that you know nothing.
> That is the meaning of true knowledge.
> **—Socrates in: https://**
> **www.brainyquote.com**

The oldest and still the most powerful, teaching method for creating critical thinking is the Socratic teaching method. The method gives students questions not answers. Of course, not all classes lend themselves to this type of teaching method but most classes need an element of teacher generated questions for the students to wrestle with. If students are passive all the time their learning and retention of information goes down. The benefits of the Socratic method is that students develop skills in thinking, reasoning, analysing, and applying the information presented by the teacher. Where it is appropriate in the cultural context that people live in, a teacher should generate classroom discussion by having a good set of questions that cause students to think and apply the material being taught.

A teacher using the Socratic method should:

- Keep the questions focused on the topic at hand.
- Keep the discussion lively.
- Include as many of the students as possible in the discussion.

- Draw in shy students with questions directed to them. It is better to thank them for their responses and ask good follow up questions that will cause them to think more deeply and arrive at more accurate conclusions.
- Listen to the student's answers.
- Do not condemn any student responses to the questions.
- Give students the freedom to speak without fear of judgment.
- Add some humour where appropriate.
- Summarize at the end and draw the student's thoughts and comments together into clear conclusion.

The Socratic Method is a real departure from the teacher-centred method of lecturing. Lecturing is appropriate in some courses such as biblical languages and research. However, on the higher levels of teaching a teacher should use more of the Socratic Method.

On the bachelor's degree level of teaching a teacher can use the Socratic Method to a lesser degree but should still introduce the students to the method. Someone might argue that the bachelor's level students do not know that much. This may be true but they still have experiences. For example, a student may not have ever studied the theology of prayer but the student certainly has prayed many times both privately and publicly. You are dialoguing with their experience more that their knowledge.

On the master's degree level, the Socratic Method should be used more as master's level students have both knowledge and experience. This knowledge and experienced should be used by the teacher to deepen the student's understanding of the topic and sharpen their thinking.

On the doctoral degree level, the Socratic Method should be a common practice. Doctoral students have vast experience and that should be used by the teacher.

> If you are giving a graduate course you don't try to impress the students with oratory, you try to challenge them, get them to question you.
>
> **—Norm Chomsky in: https://www.brainyquote.com**

In the Socratic Method, students need to think about the questions posed by the teacher, formulate an answer, share the answer to the rest of the class and be able to defend his or her answer to the question.

> The goal of the Socratic Method is to help students process information and engage in deeper understanding of topics. Most importantly, Socratic teaching engages students in dialogue and discussion that is collaborative and open-minded as opposed to debate, which is often competitive and individualized. Ideally, teachers develop open-ended questions about texts and encourage students to use textual evidence to support their opinions and answers.
>
> —http://www.learnnc.org/lp/pages/4994

Conclusion

Teaching is both an art and a science. Each cultural context, each teacher and each course being taught will determine which of the methods of teaching from this chapter should be used. Variety should be the style of all teachers as they seek to develop students for their careers. To be a deductive teacher is good. To be an inductive teacher is good. To be a Socratic teacher is good. If someone introduced me at a seminar as "Inductive and Socratic," I would be happy as this is what I am as a teacher.

Study Questions

1. Explain the difference between the inductive and deductive teaching methods.
2. What are some characteristics of a Socratic teacher?
3. Will the Socratic Method be usable in your cultural context? Explain your answer.

CHAPTER 13

INFORMATION VS. TRANSFORMATION

In this chapter, two different teaching approaches will be considered. One is teaching for information and the other is teaching for transformation. Both are valid methods for classroom communication.

Teaching for Information

You have heard that we are in the information age. This refers to the fact that we have unlimited access to information on the Internet. Just choose the topic you want to research, go to the Internet and then get your information free. However, this chapter is more concerned about classroom information. What is teaching for information? How does a teacher teach for information? What are the strengths and weaknesses of informational teaching?

What is teaching for information?

Teaching for information can also be called teacher-centered teaching, lecturer-based teaching, classical teaching or transactional teaching. Teacher-centred teaching was covered in a previous chapter. Lecture-based information is teaching which follows the traditional historic way of presenting or reading a paper in class.

Classical education depends on a three-part process of training the mind. The early years of school are spent in absorbing facts, and systematically laying the foundations for advanced study. In the middle grades, students learn to think through arguments. In the high school years, they learn to express themselves.

—https://en.wikipedia.org/wiki/
Classical_education_movement

Transactional teaching involves the transmission of knowledge from teacher to student. Students are expected to simply assimilate and synthesize the new knowledge on their own.

—http://www.columbia.edu/cu/tat/pdfs/Transformational
%20Teaching.pdf

Transactional teaching works best for certain courses such as Greek, Hebrew, research, computers and mathematics.

> New information makes new and fresh ideas possible.
>
> **—Zig Ziggler in: https://
> www.brainyquote.com**

Information teaching lays the foundation for all other educational experiences. Information becomes the base for all further discussions and classroom interactions. The Bible gives examples of the need for God's people to have a base of information. For example, the Prophet Hosea says in 4:6 *My people are destroyed from a lack of knowledge.*

Educators and public leaders like to quote this verse, but all too frequently, they are unaware of what is meant by knowledge in this passage. It is not scientific, secular, or technical knowledge that is meant, but religious knowledge, the knowledge of God

> through his revealed will, the Bible; and even more than this is
> meant; it means conformity to the will of God.
> —https://www.studylight.org/commentary/hosea/4-6.html

A lack of knowledge of God can lead to destruction through ignorance. Teaching information has a place in the Christian life. There were times when God needed to give his people information. In the Old Testament, the Law is an example of information. The information that was given to Moses was passed down orally and codified in Rabbinical Judaism. The construction of the tabernacle and temple were examples of a lot of information being passed onto God's people. It was information of a specific nature and was not open to debate until a later time. Jesus' teaching on the Sermon on the Mount is a form of teaching for information. Note that the disciples did not debate Jesus' teachings. Jesus was laying down critical information for his people to learn. Dr. Ben Carson writes,

> There is so much potential out there in young people and they
> aren't getting the right information or being encouraged in the
> right ways. This is our duty as a society.
> —Ben Carson in: https://www.brainyquote.com

How does a teacher teach for information?

Teaching for information is important. But how do we do it effectively? Suggestions are as follows:

- The traditional lecture. The traditional lecture is a commonly used way of teaching and transferring information from the teacher to the student. It is teacher-centred whereby the teacher does all the talking and conveying of important information.
- Bible memory. Bible memory is a good way to learn Bible information. Hide God's Word in your heart for success later in life as it is needed.

- Memorization. Memorization of certain subjects is a good way to learn information. Examples would be learning Greek and Hebrew. Once you master the alphabet you can begin to master vocabulary and grammar.
- Writing. Writing out various lists helps students to learn information. For example, in Bible school students would write out the names of the books of the Bible. Or they would write out the names of Israelite kings in the Old Testament.
- Reading. Reading is a good way of absorbing information. Teachers assign readings to help students get new information.

Some advantages of informational teaching are, firstly, that they can cover a lot more material than discussion based teaching. Second, it is less stressful on the teacher. To read a set of notes, or to simply lecture, is less stress than planning for student discussions. Third, it is easier to test students on what you taught them. Fourth, it is easier to control the class and keep student's attention. Fifth, a teacher who has mastered his or her subject has a lot to share from their wealth of experience and research.

Ezra, after returning from Babylon to Jerusalem gave a good example of informational teaching.

For Ezra had devoted himself to the study and observance of the Law of the Lord, and to teaching its decrees and laws in Israel.

—Ezra 7:10

One of the great joys of life is creativity. Information goes in, gets shuffled about, and comes out in new and interesting ways.
—Peter McWilliams in: https:// www.brainyquote.com

Information based teaching is good for certain subjects and contexts. When teaching new students or teaching brand new subjects, a measure of informational teaching is necessary.

Teaching for Transformation

A second approach to teaching is called transformational teaching. It is often applied to teaching children but has application to teaching on the Bible College and seminary levels as well. A number of scholarly quotes describe transformational teaching.

> We define transformational pedagogy as an act of teaching designed to change the learner academically, socially, and spiritually. Transformational teaching begins with the learner, and transformational learning involves deep understanding and occurs in classrooms where teachers have high expectations.[1]
>
> Transformational teaching emphasizes inquiry, critical thinking, and the development of higher-order thinking and communication skills. Teaching Strategies requires a fresh approach to teaching and learning. It must adopt a learner-centered rather than an instructor centered approach.
>
> —http://www.columbia.edu/cu/tat/pdfs/Transformational %20Teaching.pdf

> The growth and development of people is the highest calling of leadership.
> **—Harvey S. Firestone in: https:// www.brainyquote.com**

Successful teaching involves much more than the transmission of content and skills. Our ultimate goal is to create

---

[1]Rosebrough p.16

independent, self-directed, self-motivated learners who are capable of critiquing and directing their own work; who are open to alternative viewpoints; and who have strongly developed higher order thinking skills. At its best, teaching is a developmental process in which a student moves from less to more sophisticated ideas and abilities. In addition to teaching subject matter and methods, we have a more expansive goal: To create reflective, self-critical learners, who understand our discipline's goals, who have internalized our profession's standards, and who have high-level skills in interpretation, analysis, and communication. As an instructor, one of your most important tasks is to guide, motivate, and assist your students through this maturational process. Students must recognize the limitations of their current skills, knowledge, and perspectives. They must realize that approaches rewarded in school–such as rote memorization, the mechanical use of formulas, or the parroting back of ideas from a textbook— are no longer sufficient in college, where we value originality, high-level analytical skills, and facility in writing.

—http://www.columbia.edu/cu/tat/pdfs/Transformational %20Teaching.pdf

The Apostle Paul was a transformational teacher. This is based on what he said to the Christians in Rome in Romans 12:2,

> *Do not conform to the pattern of this world, but be transformed by the renewing of your mind. Then you will be able to test and approve what God's will is—his good, pleasing and perfect will.*

Paul says you are transformed by the renewing of your mind. What does that mean?

> Through our bodies we express what we think, what we have and how we live. This renewing is an internal process, a reorientation of our worldview as we seek to live the way

Christ lived and to think as he thought. By offering our bodies to God, we are offering him our minds. Only when we live this transformed life will we be able to please God and discover and enjoy God's perfect will.

—Kasali p.1368 in: ABC

Christians are transformed when their minds are renewed. Transformation begins with the mind. Teachers influence the mind. How? We influence the mind by what we teach and what we are as a person. We are to look at students holistically and not one dimensionally.

> The mere imparting of information is not education.
> **—Carter G. Woodson in: https:// www.brainyquote.com**

Principles of transformational teaching

According to Rosebrough (p.9) there are eight principles of transformational teaching. They are;

- Inspire your students.

Great teachers inspire their students to live for greater purposes. Jesus said statements like, *Seek first the Kingdom of God*. He said, *Go into all the world and make disciples*. He said, *Lift up your eyes unto the fields which are white unto harvest.* Inspiring teachers teach to higher purposes. They teach to the head but also to the heart. Inspiring teachers teach holistically. This means to teach academically (the brain), socially (create community), and spiritually (for God's glory).

- Embrace your role as a whole teacher.

Be an academic teacher but also be a community-minded teacher. Create community in the classroom by group exercises and discussion times. Create a climate of spirituality. Have a class devotion at the beginning. Pray with the students. One time, at the end of a course, I asked students what they liked most about the course. One student said he liked the devotional the best. Jesus taught information but usually applied his teaching to the lives of the disciples.

- Teach the whole student.

The whole student is more than the brain. Engage the spirit in class. Be like Jesus who taught, prayed and sent the 70 out on assignment.

- Place students in the center.

Schools exist for students. What are the needs of the students? They usually need academic teaching, skills development, spiritual growth and encouragement. As a teacher, it is important to remember that these are people who will be our pastors, teachers and leaders in the near future. Be a pastor to the class members.

- Teach for learning.

To teach for learning means to help students wrestle with problems and come up with solutions. This will work for most classes. It means some sacrifice of time away from teaching information but in the end, it is worth it. Find out what students already know and what their hopes are for the class you are teaching.

- Know how students learn.

Dr. Rosebrough writes,

> Good teaching demands that we use our heads and hearts. We employ our minds to understand how learners learn. We use our hearts to understand why we are teaching, to create a classroom environment that prizes learns and to instil confidence in students that they can be transformed by the experience of learning.
>
> —p. 96

- Teach students how to learn.

Do not assume that students know how to learn. Give clear instructions on all reading and writing assignments. What do you want from them in papers and exams? Use variety in your teaching by using active (group work, presentations, question and answer) and passive (reading, note taking) learning opportunities.

- Teach by asking questions.

Questions make learning active. Problem solving makes learning active. Guided inquiry makes learning active. Be sure and accept all answers students say without being judgmental. If a student gives a wrong answer, rather than correcting the student, ask the class what they think of the answer.

Dr. Jeffrey D. Curtis shares, from a pastor's perspective what church based spiritual transformation includes. It can also be applied to Bible College and seminary level teaching. Dr. Curtis writes,

> It is critical that churches provide a context in which each element of biblical faith can be nurtured. Only in such context can spiritual transformation take place. Churches can help create this environment of change by including the following elements in their Bible study groups:

1. The Bible is the sole authority for life.
2. Transformation is the goal, not merely transferring information.
3. The teacher leads the members to discover truths on their own, rather than conveying all information through lecture.
4. You recognize that children, youth, and adults learn in different ways and on different levels. Teachers must adjust their teaching methods to fit the style and level of the class.
5. The teacher leads the members to think, examine, and express how the truth of the Scripture relates to their lives.
6. The class plans actions to carry out the truths of the Scripture.
7. Group members are led to share what God has done in their lives through transformational Bible study.
8. The class engages in member-to-member discussion and group interaction.
9. The teacher is being transformed himself/herself.
10. Teaching is bathed in prayer and the power of the Holy Spirit is present.

—http://www.lifeway.com/Article/pastors-transform-christian-education

Conclusion

Information will help students to begin their journey of growth but our goal or vision as teachers is the transformation of students to a more complete maturity in the Christian life. Information lays the foundation for transformation to take place. Truthful information is key to laying a solid foundation for transformation to take place.

The Apostle Paul put it this way,

> *And we all, who with unveiled faces contemplate the Lord's glory, are being transformed into his image with ever-increasing glory, which comes from the Lord, who is the Spirit.*
>
> —2 Corinthians 3:18

Holistic transformation means growing in maturity including academically, socially and spiritually. Teachers need to be transformational in order to see their students transformed into the likeness of Christ.

Study Questions

1. What are two goals of transformational teaching?
2. How is transformational teaching different than informational teaching?
3. Is transformational teaching realistic for a church setting? Explain your answer.

CHAPTER 14

TEACHING FOR SPIRITUAL FORMATION

Some seminaries are noted for their academics. Some are known for their emphasis on missions. Some focus on prayer. However, the overriding priority for all Bible Colleges and seminaries should be spiritual formation. Seminaries and Bible Colleges ought not to lock onto one of the above priorities as specialists but be more of a generalist paying attention to all of them while emphasizing spiritual formation.

Three curriculum priorities for all seminaries and Bible schools should be an emphasis on academics, Christian service, and spiritual formation. Bible study falls under academics. Skills development falls under service. Worship falls under spiritual formation. Spiritual growth refers to a wider scope of growth, which can include Bible knowledge and skills development. Spiritual formation focuses more on the development of our relationship with God and aspects of the Christian walk.

What is Spiritual formation?

Let us look at several quotes on what spiritual formation is. Additional light will be shed on each definition to help clarify the author's intent.

> Christian spiritual formation refers to the intentional communal process of growing in our relationship with God and becoming conformed to Christ through the power of the Holy Spirit.
>
> —Wilhoit 2008. p.23

- Christian: By Christian, we mean true followers of Jesus Christ who have been born-again.

- Intentional: Intentional means it is not something that will happen automatically. As Christian leaders, we need to aim for spiritual growth.

- Communal: Spiritual growth often happens in the church as iron sharpens iron.

- Process of growing: Growth is a process. A tree does not shoot up to full size overnight. In the same way, spiritual growth is a day-to-day experience.

- Relationship with God: Intensifying our relationship with God is a main goal of spiritual formation.

- Conformed to Christ: Christ is our example and spiritual formation helps us to conform to him.

- Through the Holy Spirit: The Holy Spirit is key to our being formed in the likeness of Jesus Christ.

Dr. Wilhoit has a second definition of spiritual formation. It is similar to his first definition but adds to the clarification of the definition:

> Christian spiritual formation: (1) is intentional; (2) is communal; (3) requires our engagement; (4) is accomplished by the Holy Spirit; (5) is for the glory of God and the service of others; and (6) has as its means and end the imitation of Christ.
>
> —Wilhoit 2008. p.23

He adds to the first definition "for the glory of God." Our growth is ultimately for the higher purpose of God's glory. Second, he adds that spiritual formation has a purpose for the service of others. We cannot minister to others if the Holy Spirit has not ministered to us. Finally, he adds that spiritual formation is to help us imitate Christ in all that we do.

> Sanctification is the work of the Holy Spirit in us whereby our inner being is progressively changed, freeing us more and more from sinful traits and developing with us over time the virtues of Christ like character.
>
> **—Jerry Bridges in: https://www.brainyquote.com**

A third definition of spiritual formation comes from Bruce Demarest. He defines spiritual formation as follows:

> Spiritual formation concerns the shaping of our life after the pattern or Jesus Christ. It is a process that takes place in the inner person, whereby the Spirit reshapes our character. Many Scriptures describe this lifelong process of spiritual formation, including 2 Corinthians 3:18; Galatians 4:19; Ephesians 4:13, 22-24; Colossians 3:9-10; and 1 Thessalonians 5:23.
>
> —Wilhoit. 2008. p.188

Those verses which are given in the above quote to give a biblical basis for the definition are as follows:

- *And we all, who with unveiled faces contemplate the Lord's glory, are being transformed into his image with ever-increasing glory, which comes from the Lord, who is the Spirit.*

  —2 Corinthians 3:18

- *My dear children, for whom I am again in the pains of childbirth until Christ is formed in you,*

  —Galatians 4:19

- *.. until we all reach unity in the faith and in the knowledge of the Son of God and become mature, attaining to the whole measure of the fullness of Christ.*

  —Ephesians 4:13

- *You were taught, with regard to your former way of life, to put off your old self, which is being corrupted by its deceitful desires; 22 to be made new in the attitude of your minds; 24 and to put on the new self, created to be like God in true righteousness and holiness.*

  —Ephesians 4:22-24

- *Do not lie to each other, since you have taken off your old self with its practices 10 and have put on the new self, which is being renewed in knowledge in the image of its Creator.*

  —Colossians 3:9-10

- *May God himself, the God of peace, sanctify you through and through. May your whole spirit, soul and body be kept blameless at the coming of our Lord Jesus Christ.*

  —1 Thessalonians 5:23

"Grace to You," the online ministries of Grace Community Church USA, explains spiritual formation in the following terms

> In broad terms, spiritual formation is the process of spiritual shaping and growth. In Christian circles, spiritual formation refers to more than mere academic instruction. Most often, it is a reference to the dynamic means of sanctification. It deals with

the ongoing work of the Holy Spirit and the various methods
He used to bring about spiritual growth in our lives.
—https://www.gty.org/library/blog/B120910/what-is-
spiritual-formation-and-why-does-it-matter

A writer for the Internet website gotquestions.org writes,

True *biblical* spiritual formation, or spiritual transformation,
begins with the understanding that we are sinners living apart
from God. Our faculties have been corrupted by sin so that
we cannot please God. True spiritual transformation occurs as
we yield ourselves to God so that He may transform us by the
guidance and power of the Holy Spirit.
—https://www.gotquestions.org/spiritual-formation.html

In summary, with the above writers, this author defines spiritual
formation as the process of becoming like Christ through the
leadership of the Holy Spirit and the Word of God. Spiritual formation
takes place individually in personal study and worship and it takes place
communally through the church.

Why is Spiritual formation important?

Spiritual formation is important because in an ultimate sense we are
spiritual beings. We came from dust and we will return one day to dust.
God told Adam,

*By the sweat of your brow you will eat your food until you return
to the ground, since from it you were taken; for dust you are and to
dust you will return.*

—Genesis 3:19

Only our spirit survives the death experience. Our bodies return to the
earh. Solomon said in Ecclesiastes 12:6-7,

*Remember him—before the silver cord is severed,
  and the golden bowl is broken;*

> *before the pitcher is shattered at the spring,*
> *and the wheel broken at the well,*
> *and the dust returns to the ground it came from,*
> *and the spirit returns to God who gave it.*

Therefore, the development of the spirit is critical. Paul says it is more important to train the spirit than to exercise the body. Paul wrote to Timothy,

> *For physical training is of some value, but godliness has value for all things, holding promise for both the present life and the life to come.*
> —1 Timothy 4:8

> True spiritual transformation occurs as we yield ourselves to God so that He may transform us by the guidance and power of the Holy Spirit. At least half of every New Testament epistle is geared toward how to live a life well pleasing to God— by obedience and submission to the Holy Spirit in all things. Scripture does not only call us the redeemed, saved, saints, sheep, soldiers, and servants, but teaches us that only through the power of the Spirit can we live up to what the names mean.
> —https://www.gotquestions.org/spiritual-formation.html

Spiritual formation is important as it is the process of becoming more like Christ and enjoying the relationship that it brings. The Apostle Paul wrote,

> *For whom he did foreknow, he also did predestinate to be conformed to the image of his Son, that he might be the firstborn among many brethren.*
>
> —Romans 8:29

How do we teach for Spiritual formation?

Both human and divine teachers are involved in teaching spiritual formation. The New Testament is full of human teachers; Paul, Peter,

Timothy, Apollos and many others. Divine teachers are also operative such as Jesus and the Holy Spirit. Paul in 1Corinthians tells us how the human and divine teachers work together. *I planted the seed, Apollos watered it, but God has been making it grow* (1 Corinthians 3:6).

Our teaching methods need to be linked to the goals of spiritual formation. What are the goals of these teachers in terms of spiritual formation?

- Being like Christ. *I want to know Christ—yes, to know the power of his resurrection and participation in his sufferings, becoming like him in his death* (Philippians 3:10).
- Grow in the grace and knowledge of Jesus Christ. *But grow in the grace and knowledge of our Lord and Saviour Jesus Christ. To him be glory both now and forever! Amen* (2 Peter 3:18).
- *Be transformed by the renewing of your mind.* Romans 12:2.
- Be transformed into his image.

> *And we all, who with unveiled faces contemplate the Lord's glory,*
> *are being transformed into his image with ever-increasing glory,*
> *which comes from the Lord, who is the Spirit.*
>
> —2 Corinthians 3:18

- Equipped for service. *To equip his people for works of service, so that the body of Christ may be built up* (Ephesians 4:12).

We acknowledge that true spiritual formation is a work of the Holy Spirit. Nevertheless, as we stated earlier, the human being also plays a role. Several writers have commented on the human part or responsibility of spiritual formation:

> The five facets of spiritual formation, then, are: *reflective reading, active repentance, total stewardship, penetrating prayer, and community accountability.* As we consider specific practices that

aid in formation, it is essential to be prepared to surrender time. Spiritual formation cannot be found in a "Five Minutes to Improved Spirituality" product. Be prepared to change the pattern of your life to practice the purposes of God.

—http://www.christianitytoday.com/biblestudies/articles/spiritualformation/beingformed.html

From the Christian Research Network the writer suggests that the following spiritual disciplines can aid us in spiritual formation:

Meditation, prayer, fasting, study, simplicity, solitude, submission, service, confession, worship, guidance, celebration.

—http://christianresearchnetwork.org/topic/spiritual-formation/

This author suggests the following for how to teach for spiritual formation:

1. Set high spiritual goals. Jesus in John 4:23-24 says we are to worship in *spirit and truth.* Jesus comments that the church is to be a *house of prayer* (Matthew 21:13). In John 8:32 Jesus says we can know the truth, which sets you free. These are high goals to strive for.

2. Teachers are to model the Christ-life. Have a class devotion and a humble attitude. Be like Christ. Be a servant leader. Paul said in 1 Corinthians 11:1, *Follow my example, as I follow the example of Christ.*

3. Be prayed up for every class. Pray ahead by putting prayer "in the bank."

4. Rely on the work of the Holy Spirit (John 14:26).

5. Not pastor-teacher but teacher-pastor (Ephesians 5:11-12).

6. Share your spiritual journey.

So we cared for you. Because we loved you so much, we were
delighted to share with you not only the gospel of God but our
lives as well.

—1 Thessalonians 2:8

The role of the Holy Spirit in spiritual formation.

The Holy Spirit is the key to success in spiritual formation. Scriptures
that emphasize the role of the Holy Spirit are as follows

- *But the Advocate, the Holy Spirit, whom the Father will send in my*
  name, will teach you all things and will remind you of everything
  I have said to you.

  —John 14:26

- *This is what we speak, not in words taught us by human wisdom*
  but in words taught by the Spirit, explaining spiritual realities
  with Spirit-taught words.

  —1 Corinthians 2:13

- *To these four young men God gave knowledge and understanding*
  of all kinds of literature and learning.

  —Daniel 1:17

- *Because our gospel came to you not simply with words but also*
  with power, with the Holy Spirit and deep conviction. You know
  how we lived among you for your sake.

  —1 Thessalonians 1:5

Since we are spiritual beings, it is only logical that the Spirit of God is
the main "Professor" as spiritual students.

> Only the Holy Spirit, the Spirit of the Lord,
> can transform us.
> — **Joseph Prince in: https://
> www.brainyquote.com**

Signs of spiritual formation

How do we know if spiritual formation is taking place? What signs can we see in people if our programme of spiritual formation is taking place or not? Signs of spiritual formation taking place can be seen in a person's growing commitment to the two instructions that Jesus gave to us. The first is the Great Commandment.

> *Jesus replied: "Love the Lord your God with all your heart and with all your soul and with all your mind." [38]This is the first and greatest commandment. [39]And the second is like it: "Love your neighbour as yourself." [40]All the Law and the Prophets hang on these two commandments.*
>
> —Matthew 22:37-40

Is someone's love for God growing and is a person's love towards their neighbour growing? A second sign that a person is experiencing spiritual growth and formation is a person's commitment to the Great Commission.

> *Therefore go and make disciples of all nations, baptizing them in the name of the Father and of the Son and of the Holy Spirit, [20]and teaching them to obey everything I have commanded you. And surely I am with you always, to the very end of the age.*
>
> —Matthew 28:19-20

Is someone making disciples? Are they teaching Christians to obey the commands that Jesus gave? Are they going into all the world? These are two signs of a person's growing spiritual formation.

A third sign that a person is growing spiritually is their attitude towards others. Paul in Galatians 5:22-26 says,

> *But the fruit of the Spirit is love, joy, peace, forbearance, kindness, goodness, faithfulness, gentleness and self-control. Against such things there is no law. Those who belong to Christ Jesus have crucified the flesh with its passions and desires. Since we live by the Spirit, let us keep in step with the Spirit. Let us not become conceited, provoking and envying each other.*

How we treat others is a mark of our growth in spiritual formation.

Conclusion

Spiritual formation is a goal that visionary teachers and pastors should strive for. We are spiritual beings and have access to God's teaching agenda through the Holy Spirit. Both God and man play a part in spiritual formation. Let us teach and live in the belief that God will help Christ to be formed in us (Galatians 4:19). The result of Christ being formed in us is a life committed to the glory of God and following the convictions of the Holy Spirit and obedience to the commissions that Jesus gave us. Amen.

Study Questions

1.   What is spiritual formation?
2.   Is spiritual formation different than spiritual growth?
3.   What is the role of the Holy Spirit in spiritual formation?

CHAPTER 15

A VISION FOR ACTION

All of our educational efforts should result in application to student's lives. Second, our teaching should result in action. Our lesson plans have not succeeded if the information only sits in the student's brains. A visionary teacher is concerned about how the lesson is applied to student's lives and creating actions.

> The great aim of education is not knowledge but action.
>
> **—Herbert Spence in: https:// www.brainyquote.com**

The Russian writer Anton Chekhov writes, "Knowledge is of no value unless you put it into practice." (www.brainyquote.com). I would prefer to say knowledge is of low value unless you put it into practice. Some knowledge lays a foundation for other teachings to be applied. In this chapter we will focus on the importance of action-based knowledge and teaching.

The Bible would agree that the aim of education is not knowledge for knowledge sake, but application to our lives. For example:

Be doers of the word not hearers only.

—James 1:22

Whatever you have learned or received or heard from me, or seen in me—put it into practice. And the God of peace will be with you.

—Philippians 4:9

For we are God's handiwork, created in Christ Jesus to do good works, which God prepared in advance for us to do.

—Ephesians 2:10

These are action verses for the application of teaching and knowledge to the lives of our students.

This chapter will look at several types of educational action words. We will look at:

1. Developmentalism.
2. Experiential learning.
3. Practicum.
4. Competency.
5. Outcomes.

Developmentalism

Developmentalism grew out of the over-emphasis on knowledge as being the sole purpose of education. Developmentalism often focuses on children and their development. The Bible has an example of this, *And Jesus grew in wisdom and stature, and in favour with God and man* (Luke 2:52). However, the principles of developmentalism can be applied to adult teaching as well.

Several characteristics of developmental teaching are as follows:

• Pursue one's authentic interests in community with others.

- Create learning opportunities, joint and individual projects, field trips.
- Real life learning opportunities relevant to the student's interests and needs.
- Life-long self-directed learning, and authentic participation in community life.

—http://gayleturner.net/philosophies_chart.html

One of the main proponents of developmentalism is Dr. John Dewey.

> Education, therefore, is a process of living and not a preparation for future living.
> —**John Dewey in: https://www.brainyquote.com**

John Dewey was born in 1859 in the USA. He became a noted educator and one of the most influential educators of the 20th century. He is often called the "father of the progressive education movement." The progressive movement in education places strong emphasis on problem solving and critical thinking. Group work and the development of social skills is also emphasized.

The influential twentieth-century philosopher-educator John Dewey complained that educators were constantly guilty of 'either-or thinking.' Instead of recognizing the need for both experience and educational content in schools, he said these writers tended to emphasize one at the expense of the other.[1]

---

[1]Wilhoit 2008. p.17

> Dewey's concept of education put a premium on meaningful activity in learning and participating in classroom democracy. Unlike earlier models of teaching, which relied on authoritarianism and rote learning, progressive education asserted that students must be invested in what they were learning. Dewey argued that curriculum should be relevant to student's lives. He saw learning by doing and development of practical life skills as crucial to education.
>
> —http://www.pbs.org/onlyateacher/john.html

Dewey emphasized the importance of balancing knowledge as well as the interests and experiences of the students. He pushed for a hands-on style of education without discounting the importance of knowledge. He believed that the best learning was through doing.

Christian author Dr. Richard Leyda says of Dewey,

> Dewey's concept of the role of experience in the growth of the person and his insights about learning and problem-solving methods contribute toward a more comprehensive understanding and practice of Christian education.
>
> —Leyda in: Anthony 2001. p.203

The Bible has much to say about a teacher and his or her emphasis on experience. In the Sermon on the Mount, Jesus spoke of the importance of experience:

> *Therefore everyone who hears these words of mine and puts them into practice is like a wise man who built his house on the rock.*
>
> —Matthew 7:24

Jesus was saying hearing is one thing but doing, experience, is another.

Experiential learning

Experiential learning applies the lesson to the student's lives. Students are called upon to do something with the lessons they are learning.

This can be very time consuming but beneficial in driving the lesson deeper into student's experience.

> Education, therefore, is a process of living and not a preparation for future living.
> **—Clarence Day in: https://www.brainyquote.com**

The noted educational thinker behind experiential learning is Dr. David Kolb. Kolb is an American educator born in 1939. He built his theory on previous philosophers such as John Dewey, Kurt Lewin and Jean Piaget. For Kolb, the process of experiential learning is as follows:

1. Concrete experience or "Do."

   The first stage, concrete experience (CE), is where the learner actively experiences an activity such as a lab session or fieldwork.

2. Reflective observation or "Observe."

   The second stage, reflective observation (RO), is when the learner consciously reflects back on that experience.

3. Abstract conceptualization or "Think."

   The third stage, abstract conceptualization (AC), is where the learner attempts to conceptualize a theory or model of what is observed.

4. Active experimentation or "Plan."

   The fourth stage, active experimentation (AE), is where the learner is trying to plan how to test a model or theory or plan for a forthcoming experience.

—https://www.learning-theories.com/experiential-learning-kolb.html

The central notion of Kolb's model is that learning requires both a pool of experience and some transformation of that experience into knowledge.

—Harley Atkinson in *The Evangelical Dictionary of Christian Education.* p.395

More can be studied about David Kolb's understanding of experiential teaching online and in educational philosophy books.

Christian author Dr. Henry Blackaby writes;

Knowing God through experience is radically different than knowing about God from a theology textbook. Biblical knowledge always involves experience.

—Blackaby p.68

Jesus wanted to teach Peter about who he, Jesus, was. He could have lectured Peter about his power but he chose to let Peter experience his power. Luke records:

He (Jesus) got into one of the boats, the one belonging to Simon, and asked him to put out a little from shore. Then he sat down and taught the people from the boat. When he had finished speaking, he said to Simon, "Put out into deep water, and let down the nets for a catch." Simon answered, "Master, we've worked hard all night and haven't caught anything. But because you say so, I will let down the nets." When they had done so, they caught such a large number of fish that their nets began to break.

—Luke 5:3-6

Jesus did not give Peter a lecture on fishing but told to push out into the water. Peter did that and experienced Jesus in a way he never could have from Jesus lecturing him.

Jesus was the master of experiential learning. He could have given the twelve disciples information that one day they would be able to cast out demons and heal people in Jesus' Name but he chose to send them out so they could experience the truths of Jesus' teachings. Matthew tells the story:

> *Jesus called his twelve disciples to him and gave them authority to drive out impure spirits and to heal every disease and sickness. . . . These twelve Jesus sent out with the following instructions; "Do not go among the Gentiles or enter any town of the Samaritans. Go rather to the lost sheep of Israel. As you go, proclaim this message: 'The kingdom of heaven has come near.' Heal the sick, raise the dead, cleanse those who have leprosy, drive out demons. Freely you have received; freely give."*
>
> —Matthew 10:1, 5-8

Jesus told the disciples to experience the truth and not just hear the truth.

The advantages of experiential learning is that it solidifies the things that are taught by the teacher. When students go out on evangelism trips they experience the leading and power of God as they see the Holy Spirit lead during the outreach. Some Bible College and seminary classes lend themselves to experiential learning such as classes in church ministry, missions, evangelism and discipleship. Some classes are harder to teach experientially such as theology classes and biblical languages. A teacher will not be able to cover as much information as in a straight lecture but what is taught is better learned. Sometimes less is more, that is, less lecture and more doing. Today's teachers need to find ways, big and small, to give students experiences of what the teacher is teaching. This will stay with the students long after they graduate.

Practicum

Most Bible Colleges and seminaries have courses which are called Practicum, or Practica in the plural. A practicum has two parts. Part one is the information that a student needs to have before going on the practicum. A pastoral major would do several courses in church ministry in the classroom before going on a practicum. Part two is when a student is posted to a church for a set period of time to observe the church in its week-to-week activities and also to participate in the ministry of the church such as preaching, teaching Sunday school, or going on visitation. The student is then evaluated by the local pastor and visiting lecturer to observe the student in action during the practicum.

> There's a wealth of information and knowledge you can gain from sitting down with people who are successful.
>
> **—Grant Hill in: https:// www.brainyquote.com**

The apostle Paul trained Pastor Timothy. After Timothy was sent to a church, in Ephesus, Paul went and visited him in the church at Ephesus. Note the following verses:

- *Paul came to Derbe and then to Lystra, where a disciple named Timothy lived. Timothy joined Paul on his second missionary journey.*

    —Acts 16:1

- *What you heard from me, keep as the pattern of sound teaching, with faith and love in Christ Jesus. Guard the good deposit that was entrusted to you- guard it with the help of the Holy Spirit who lives in us.*

    —2 Timothy 1:13

Timothy learns information and experience from Paul during the journey.

- *As I urged you when I went into Macedonia, stay there in Ephesus so that you may command certain people not to teach false doctrines any longer.*

—1 Timothy 1:3

Timothy was left in the Ephesus church.
- Paul visits Ephesus twice; Acts 19 and 20.

A practicum can be conducted in the Bible school, seminary or church setting. A pastor can put his own selected members through a church based practicum programme.

Competency

Competencies are skills, behaviours or knowledge that students should acquire before the class is finished at the end of a semester. Students do not have to be experts in these areas but should develop minimal abilities in each area of study. In competency-based education, a teacher gives students the information they need to begin to develop competencies, skills, in the area being taught. Then the teacher gives students the opportunity to develop various skills, competencies, based on the topic being taught. Then the teacher grades the student based on his or her performance. Paul's instruction to Timothy is a good example of this process:

And the things you have heard me say in the presence of many witnesses entrust to reliable people who will also be qualified to teach others.

—2 Timothy 2:2

Here are a few examples of what competency based education would look like in schools:

- In a class on hermeneutics: *Ability to interpret Scripture.*
- In a class on homiletics: *Ability to preach a quality sermon.*
- In a class on evangelism: *Ability to share the gospel.*
- In a class on counselling: *Ability to help ♦iagnose someone problems.*
- In a class in the Old Testament: *Ability to navigate through the Ol♦ Testament Scriptures.*
- In a class in the New Testament: *Ability to explain the ♦ifferent historical contexts between Jesus an♦ Paul.*

Jesus told the disciples they would need certain competencies to perform his work. Mark tells us,

> *Jesus went up on a mountainsi♦e an♦ calle♦ to him those he wante♦, an♦ they came to him. He appointe♦ twelve that they might be with him an♦ that he might sen♦ them out to preach an♦ to have authority to ♦rive out ♦emons.*
>
> —Mark 3:13-15

The twelve listened to Jesus, got his instructions, and went out to minister.

Competency based education is simply a combination of information and skills development that are to be demonstrated by the end of the class.

Outcomes

Outcomes are observable and measurable behaviours that a student used to show that they have mastered a set of skills. For comparison, goals are general and outcomes are specific in relationship to practical skills. In outcomes-based education, a teacher states what a student should know and be able to demonstrate by the end of the course. Educational Outcomes are the skills that are developed upon which educational programmes are based. They can be defined as the skills that students will need to be successful in work, family, school, church or community. The outcomes relate to skills that can be demonstrated by the students. Some examples of a variety of outcomes are as follows:

- Preach a biblically based sermon.
- Make a disciple.
- Lead someone to Christ.
- Teach from a lesson plan.

Schools set certain general outcomes for their programmes on each degree level. For example;

1.   Bachelor (BA) degree level outcomes:
     - Be able to successfully study a passage of the Bible.
     - Preach a simple sermon.
     - Demonstrate basic research skills.
     - Lead someone to Christ.
2.   MA degree level outcomes:
     - Preach a biblically based expositional sermon.
     - Demonstrate basic Internet research skills.
     - Successfully teach a class on the BA level.
     - Demonstrate good writing skills.
3.   PhD degree level outcomes:
     - Preach a Bible passage using the Greek or Hebrew.
     - Demonstrate the use of high quality Internet research.
     - Be able to use English grammar and composition skilfully.
     - Excellence in leading classroom discussions.

The Bible has outcomes which can be demonstrated for all Christians such as:

1.   Pray without ceasing.

2.   Go into all the world and make disciples.

3.   Go into all the world and preach the gospel.

4.   Preach in season and out of season.

5.   Take care of widows and orphans.

6.   Husbands love your wives as Christ loved the church.

The Bible has many more outcomes that we strive for but the ones listed above are key to the success of Christian living.

Conclusion

The discipline of education has many ways of approaching the task of teaching and equipping students for a victorious life and ministry. Students in Bible Colleges and seminaries are on the way to full time ministry and need to be equipped for the task. The equipping includes outstanding teaching of information and knowledge as a foundation for other learning tasks. The equipping includes a godly example of the spiritual life in prayer and love towards God. It includes the development of skills through good teaching, prayer, experiential learning, and the development of competencies for ministry.

The best teachers are ones that have a vision for the subject matter at hand, the students, and God. These three aspects of teaching will bring great satisfaction and fulfillment to the teacher and produce a group of graduates who will go out and change the world. My desire is that one day your students will say the same thing about you that the people who listened to Jesus said,

> *When Jesus had finished saying these things, the crowds were amazed at his teaching, because he taught as one who had authority, and not as their teachers of the law.*
>
> —Matthew 7:28-29

Amen.

Study Questions

1. What is the role of experience in teaching?
2. Write out a plan for a practicum for your department.
3. What is the difference between competences and outcomes?

BIBLIOGRAPHY

Anthony, Michael J. *Christian Education for the 21st Century*. Grand Rapids, MI. Baker, 2001.

__________. *The Evangelical Dictionary of Christian Education*. Grand Rapids, MI. Baker, 2001.

Blackaby, Henry and Richard Blackaby. *Experiencing God Day by Day*. B&H Publishing Group. Nashville, TN, 2006.

Draper, Edythe. *Draper's Book of Quotations for the Christian World*. Wheaton, Illinois: Tyndale House, 1992.

Downs, Perry. *Teaching for Spiritual Growth: An Introduction to Christian Education*. Grand Rapids, Michigan: Zondervan, 1994.

Fafunwa, A. Babs. *History of Education in Nigeria*. London: George Allen and Unwin, 1993.

Gangel, Ken. *24 Ways to Improve Your Teaching*. Eugene, Oregon. Victor Books, 1974.

__________. *The Christian Educator's Handbook on Adult Education*. Grand Rapids, MI. Baker Books, 1993.

(HCSB). *Holman Christian Standard Bible*. Nashville, Tennessee: Holman Bible Publishers, 2005.

LeFever, Marlene. *Marlene. Learning Styles: Reaching Everyone God Gave You to Teach*. Colorado Springs, CO. Cook Communications Ministries, 2004.

Lingenfelter, Judith E. and Sherwood G. Lingenfelter. *Teaching Cross-Culturally: An Incarnational Model for Learning and Teaching*. Grand Rapids Michigan USA. Baker, 2003.

McKenzie, E.C. *14,000 Quips and Quotes; for speakers, writers, editors, preachers, and teachers*. Grand Rapids, MI.: Baker Books, 1991.

(NIV). *The NIV Stuʻy Bible New International Version.* Grand Rapids, Michigan: Zondervan Bible Publishers, 1985.

Rosenbrough, Thomas R. and Ralph G. Leverett. *Transformational Teaching in the Information age.* Alexandra, VA. ASCD, 2011.

Tan, Paul Lee. *Encyclopeʻia of 7,700 Illustrations: Signs of the Times.* Rockville, Maryland: Assurance Publishers, 1985.

Wilhoit, James C. *Spiritual Formation as if the Church Matlereʻ: Growing in Christ through Community.* Grand Rapids MI.: Baker, 2008.

Tokunboh Adeyemo (General Ed.). *Africa Bible Commentary.* Nairobi, Kenya: WordAlive Publishers, 2006.